P9-DUR-388

A YEAR TO LIVE

A Year to Live

HOW TO LIVE THIS YEAR
AS IF IT WERE YOUR LAST

STEPHEN LEVINE

BELL TOWER NEW YORK

Grateful acknowledgment is made to Beacon Press, Boston, for
permission to reprint material from The Kabir Book by Robert Bly.
Copyright© 1971, 1977 by Robert Bly. Copyright© 1977 by The
Seventies Press. Reprinted by permission of Beacon Press, Boston.

Published by Bell Tower, an imprint of Harmony Books,
a division of Crown Publishers, Inc.,
201 East 50th Street, New York, New York 10022.
Member of the Crown Publishing Group.

Random House, Inc. New York, Toronto, London, Sydney, Auckland
http://www.randomhouse.com/

Bell Tower and colophon are trademarks of Crown Publishers, Inc.

Printed in the United States of America

Design by Barbara Balch

Library of Congress Cataloging-in-Publication Data

Levine, Stephen, 1937–
    A year to live : how to live this year as if it were your last /
Stephen Levine. — 1st ed.
        p.   cm.
    1. Self-actualization (Psychology).   2. Spiritual life.
3. Death—Psychological aspects.   4. Terminally ill—Psychology.
I. Title.
BF637.S4L485   1997   97-4072
170'.44—dc21   CIP

ISBN 0-517-70879-5

10 9 8 7 6, 5 4 3 2 1

First Edition

TO ONDREA,

who was with me every step of the way.
Her energy and insight permeate this book.

CONTENTS

Remember, friends, as you pass by,
As you are now so once was I.
As I am now, so you must be.
Prepare yourself to follow me.

—*Common eighteenth-century epitaph*

A YEAR TO LIVE

INTRODUCTION

This is a book of renewal. It is not simply about dying but about the restoration of the heart, which occurs when we confront our life and death with mercy and awareness. It is an opportunity to resolve our denial of death as well as our denial of life in a year-long experiment in healing, joy, and revitalization.

The program described in this book need not be followed in a linear way. Indeed, readers are encouraged to experiment and create their own timetable. For instance, the finding of one's own song and healing chant would not be left until the end of the year, even though that is where I deal with it in the book, but would be integrated, along with all the other practices, into a very personal process of healing and renewal.

CATCHING UP

WITH YOUR

LIFE

As I have accompanied the dying to the threshold over the last twenty years, it has become painfully clear how often death takes people unawares. Even those who had months or even years of illness to prepare themselves often lamented how completely unprepared they were for their death.

In their last year many people feel as if they have a second chance at growth and inner healing. Many speak of catching up with their lives just "in the nick of time." Having observed the renewal that occurs for so many people because they have been given a terminal diagnosis or because their natural wisdom inspires them to open more profoundly to life, I offer an experiment that amplifies your potential for healing by living the next year as if it were your last.

On their deathbed some people look back on their lives and are overwhelmed by a sense of failure. They have a closet full of regrets. They become disheartened when they reflect on how they have overlooked the preciousness of their relationships, forgotten the importance of finding their "true work," and delayed what some call "living my own life." Because they had left so many parts of their life for "later," they felt fragmented about unsatisfying work, unfinished business in relationships, and compromised lifestyles. But "later" came much sooner than they expected, and they found themselves burdened by unfulfilled dreams and a sense of incompleteness.

Many people, although they have few other complaints, experience a certain remorse about having neglected spiritual growth, while even more express dismay that there has been so little authentic joy in their lives. All but those who have fully opened to life say that they would live differently if they had just one more year.

We don't have to die feeling like a failure, full of shame and fear, unable to navigate by the clear light of our true heart. Indeed, that is what this book has to offer: a year to live as consciously as possible, a year to finish business, to catch up with our lives, to investigate and deal with our fear of death, to cultivate our true heart and find our essential wisdom and joy. A year to live as if that is all that remains.

Many people say that if they had another year to live they would change their work situation. Some say they would quit. Most concede that they would at the very least reduce the number of hours they work, change jobs, or perhaps study some long-admired skill even though there might be no job at the end of the rainbow. More than a few with advanced degrees say they would like to have been carpenters or stone masons. Many people speak of interests that had to be put aside because of family responsibilities, country, and social acceptability. Some, recognizing their desires, bought themselves the cello they had always wanted or the lathe, the canvas stretcher, or the new computer crammed with art programs. Many acknowledge a love of nature that they allowed to go dormant, and are drawn to long walks in the woods and sitting quietly by the sea. Some went back to church, some took up a meditation practice, turning toward the mystery, investigating wholeheartedly their own deathless nature.

One day in San Francisco, a dentist friend, while working on my teeth, told me that it was his fiftieth birthday. "Well then, just ten more years to live, to really live!" I joked through the nitrous oxide. Knowing his delight in physical sport, I floated the possibility that his body might have only another ten years of the energy and stamina necessary for his favorite endeavors, backpacking and wild-river rafting. Though I was only half-kidding, and fifty-five years old myself at the time, he was apparently ripe to hear this, and a few months later changed his office hours to a four-day week, finalized his divorce, and bought a new pair of skis. I have never seen him so lighthearted as when he speaks about how much more time he has to live by giving himself one extra day each week. Now the game is to remind him not to overbook those four days. Clearly we reclaim our lives one step at a time.

There were those with tangled and unsatisfying relationships who in their last year healed so much unfinished business, offering up their heart to that which remained disheartened and in fear of change. For some this resulted in a new living relationship, for others divorce and a whole new course to their lives. Many seemed to concentrate on expanding their horizons so as to become yet more gracious in the eyes of someone they admired; for some that was a lover or mate, for others it was God. But all of those who seemed to make the best use of a terminal prognosis began to change their relationship to relationship itself. They had a going-out-of-unfinished-business sale.

Many said they would have adopted a gentler pace of life, changed their surroundings, been less preoccupied with social and material ambitions. Some said they would have moved to the country, some to the city; some would have built new homes, others would have torn down old ones. But almost all said that they would have slowed down and stopped to smell, if not plant, the roses.

I suspect that if many of the people I have worked with had been offered a book like this a year before they died, they would have benefited greatly and had an easier death. This book was written as a one-year experiment in consciousness renewal, intended to sharpen life and soften death "while we still have the chance." How and where the answers to these essential questions are found is the subject and object of this book.

Some, I suspect, will come to this book because of their fear of the unknown, others because they respect it. Some because they sense the remarkable potential of dying consciously, others because they dread an unconscious departure. Or perhaps it is more accurate to say that a part of us seeks relief from our fears, while another aspect causes our focus on life to intensify, to push us to look deeper into just who or what took birth and who, indeed, it is that will someday die.

Whatever our situation, the progression—sudden or gradual—is the same: to remember, to let go, and to trust the process.

For some this may be a romantic, even casual, undertaking;

a playing with death. For others this may be the sweat-soaked struggle of a lifetime attempting to catch up with itself, to pull itself together before it departs with the last breath.

For the person with AIDS, advanced cancer, ALS, or for a dying child, this is no academic exploration. It is work that needs to be undertaken now from the deepest level available. For those who refuse to accept that they are dying, a deeper truth is offered. Preparing for death is one of the most profoundly healing acts of a lifetime.

For all of us there is an approach to the seemingly unapproachable. This is the life-affirming work of learning to stay present even under difficult circumstances, to embrace mental, physical, and spiritual pain using techniques suitable for each particular level of discomfort.

This book is intended to offer a healing process that allows a gradual completion of all that lies behind and a clear-eyed entrance into whatever may lie ahead. A process of clarity, insight, and closure.

PRACTICE

DYING

S ocrates recommended that we should "always be occupied in the practice of dying." So did the Dalai Lama. Recently, when someone asked him what he would like to do next, he answered that he was fifty-eight years old and felt that it was time to complete his preparations for death.

I too am fifty-eight years old, two-thirds through an imaginary life (one-third of a lifetime from an imaginary death). When a journey is in our future, it is never too soon to check out the travel guides and customs, and to learn the language of the world approaching. And it's never too late to complete our birth. As Buddha said, "It doesn't matter how long you have forgotten, only how soon you remember."

In many cultures and spiritual traditions it is considered an act of wisdom to prepare for death throughout life. Gandhi, shot three times in the chest, repeated the name of Ram, the Lord, as he fell from his wounds. Gandhi wasn't just having a good day; he had practiced for years to be fully alive in the moment no matter what the circumstances. God was in his heart yesterday, and so he was present today.

In the Christian faith, one is prepared for death soon after the appearance of the body, baptism being a ritual water burial that heralds a new birth of the spirit. But to have "a second chance" is barely enough for most of us. We are racing against death just to complete our birth, to fulfill the heart's destiny. Most of us live half-unborn. Perhaps that is why so many have said that when they received their "one year, last year" prognosis, they felt something tighten and then release in their gut. Somehow, beyond anything they imagined might occur in such circumstances, after the fear, an unexpected sense of spaciousness arose. One person said, "As what the doctor said really sank in I could feel something very heavy begin to lift. I felt as though I was free to live my life at last. Bizarrely, life never felt so safe. Maybe I'm crazy, but I felt more freedom and love than I had in some time. In fact, I felt not as though my life was being taken away but as though it had been given back to me. I was going to die and my life was completely my own."

I wondered what this new aliveness was that we see so often in those with only a few months to live. What boundaries have been lifted so noticeably that previous hindrances to joy and mercy toward self and others melt into an increasingly expanding awareness and appreciation of the present?

Approaching a new year at the time I read the Dalai Lama's comment, it occurred to me that a New Year's Resolution Without Parallel would be to make a commitment to live my next year as if it were my last.

In Islam and Judaism, in Hinduism and Christianity, one is prepared throughout life to meet one's maker, the Great One. Even in Buddhism, where one is taught to rely more on supreme beingness than any supreme being, one practices to meet one's maker, one's self, and discover the enormous luminosity beyond the maker and the made. Though I have in many ways been preparing for death during the last forty years of practicing an openness to, and investigation of, life, never has such a one-year life experiment seemed so appropriate.

Indeed, in the many books of possible afterlives in various traditions such as the Christian *Book of Hours* or *The Tibetan Book of the Dead*, which attempt to remedy our recoiling from a three-headed demon swirling swords and holding severed heads, or face a charging tiger, one teaching is always perfectly clear: that even dying does not overcome our fear of death, that the work to be done is to be done before we drop the body. As the god-drunken poet Kabir says, "What we call salvation belongs to the time before death. / If you don't break your ropes while you are alive / do you think ghosts will do it for you afterward? . . . / What is found now is found then."

So I committed myself to living a year as though it were my last. To practice dying. To be fully alive. To investigate the dread of, and resistance to, life and death. To complete my birth before it's over. To investigate that part of myself that refuses to take birth fully, and hops about as though it still had one foot in the womb. To enter the healing I have seen so many times as miraculous growth during a final illness. To place both feet on the ground at last. To live with mercy and awareness in the midst of the consequences of love, or the lack thereof. To explore this ground, the ground of being, out of which this impermanent body and ever-changing mind originate. To cut through a lifetime of confusion and forgetfulness. To undertake a life review with gratitude and forgiveness. To explore that which holds to its suffering, and cultivate a heart that cannot be distracted even by death.

In India, when someone dies, the body is transported on a

litter by the chanting family from the home to the sacred burning grounds. The litter carries the body as the song carries the soul. Halfway to the burning ghat, the procession halts and the litter is turned about so that the head of the deceased no longer points to the house from which he has just departed but toward the home he is approaching. Just so, I felt the carrying-board under my body and the song lifting my spirit. Clearly, it was time to stop the funeral procession and to turn my corpse toward the timeless present that includes my birth as well as my death. It was time to sit by my corpse covered in sacred fire and sing the song that frees the enormous heart from so small a life. There was just enough time for a year of being fully alive.

It is said that if you're fully alive before death, you will probably be fully alive afterward. It is also said that for those who think of themselves as "spiritual," the ego wants to attend its own funeral. Therefore we must be aware of such romantic notions during the one-year life/death experiment so as to keep ourselves from getting stuck in a tar pit of self-pitying aggrandizement. We need to remember that what will die in a year's time is not our essential being but our ability to interact physically with those we love and cherish.

You might think that working with the dying would have fully prepared me for death, particularly since I have also been teaching Buddhist meditation. But during the course of my one-year experiment I realized that all I had understood about death could be experienced at a yet deeper level. It was clear that though I was exploring the fear of death, it was the fear of life that needed to be investigated first. Certainly, on a good day, I might have been able to let go into death without much of a struggle and with my heart somewhat open. But I would have been dying without a sense of having healed and completed certain aspects of my life that I was able to control through spiritual practice but that were not wholly resolved: qualities of ambition, unforgiven miscreancies, posturings of the insecure self-image, primal attachments to, and identifications with, my suffering.

So, although I might have been able to depart life without much fuss, I still would have been leaving some unfinished business behind. (It must be said that even those who die in great peace may still have remnants yet incomplete, but the heart carries them over these obstacles nonetheless. Such largesse, however, is not something I would bet my life on.) I would have been dying perhaps without drawing all the healing and insight from the teachings life had provided. It would have been a bit like planting and nurturing a tree, protecting it from storms and drought, watching it bear fruit, and then abandoning it. Taking only those few offerings that had fallen to the ground, never reaching higher to glean from the upper branches. Leaving untouched provisions that might affect whatever navigations are to come for the migrating spirit. When we die we leave our life behind. In death, whatever wisdom we have garnered from the life just past continues to light the way for the next appropriate step.

Since we ordinarily live on the surface, caught up in bodily sensations and wildly competing thoughts, drawn into external stimuli, we more often relate *from* our life than *to* it. We hardly glimpse within the subtly expanding concentric circles that ripple through the mind from each moment of experience.

But when the heart at last acknowledges how much pain there is in the mind, it turns like a mother toward a frightened child. All that remains incomplete seems somehow workable and an unmistakable joy arises at the possibility of becoming whole at last.

Because we never know whether our next breath may be our last, being prepared for the immediate unknown becomes as practical as applying for a passport while still uncertain of our destination or time of departure. Without these first steps the last steps can go badly.

And so the one-year life experiment begins. It's my last New Year's Eve. There are only 364 days left to look into Ondrea's amazingly deep eyes, to hold our children in my arms, to do what I need to do to become who I really am, to fulfill my birth.

PREPARING

TO DIE

If you had only one year to live, what would you do?

When we ask ourselves this question, myriad possibilities arise. We spin through the full range of our fantasies from orgies to monasteries and back again.

Even on first reflection it becomes painfully obvious that the psychological momentum of our approaching demise propels a heavy wind before it. In this wind tumble the fallen leaves of our abandoned dreams and thwarted melodies. It chills us to the marrow.

The question reminds us of how much we have forgotten. A part of us begins to panic at the thought that it hasn't had quite enough time to leave something valid behind. There have been so few moments when life was all it was cracked up to be. So much that might have been different had the heart not been obstructed by fear. As we begin to see where we have been absent from life, increasing possibilities audition for our approval. The heart suggests that we become more present, that we sharpen our focus.

When death, the big wind, blows out our birthday candles,

only the wish remains, and only that longing which deepens our wisdom and compassion will be of much use. As the future rapidly becomes the present, and the present condenses into the past, how do we stay fully alive each day? Something in us shudders at how unprepared it feels. We fear that we are not up to the task, and begin to wonder how we might "cram" for death. We pray that God grades on a curve, but death is not a test; it is only another opportunity to enter life wholeheartedly.

As we reflect on this life/death riddle we may be surprised at how many options it inspires. Rather than our freedom being curtailed by having just a year left, we uncover something quite unsuspected and satisfying. We discover how much more room we have for life and how many more possibilities there are to be fully alive.

When there is only a year remaining, our options expand exponentially. Should we go on vacation: take three Barbies, a Ken, and a bottle of tequila and head for Acapulco? (Actually, I've known very few who tried this particular scenario.) Should we "get down to work" or quit our job? And what indeed does "get down to work" mean? Should we get married? Should we get divorced? Should we take up macramé? Change our religion? Become Catholic, Buddhist, Jewish, Hindu, Sufi, pregnant? Change our sex? Get a tattoo or remove one? (Lenny Bruce mused about what might happen to his body after he died, because the tattoo on his arm precluded his burial in an Orthodox Jewish cemetery. He suggested they bury most of his body in the Orthodox cemetery and place his arm in "a place of Gentile rest.") Should we read all those books we kept meaning to read? Look for a guru, leave a guru? Get a face-lift, start wearing cosmetics, stop using them, consider cryonics? Save all our money for our heirs, or spend every cent on an ex-

tended vacation? Or just try to beat the odds by killing ourselves?

The alternative—completing our birth before we die, becoming truly whole rather than just appearing to "have it together"—is more difficult. As I have often noted, those who
insist they've got their "shit together" are usually standing in it
at the time.

There are as many different responses to a terminal prognosis as there are personalities and points of view, much less
philosophies about death.

Sometimes it takes a journey to come home. We may even
have to leave our comfortable (though always only rented,
never owned) domicile to do it. Life is like that and so is death.

Thus, in the one-year experiment, we may keep our jobs,
our mates, and our children and not trade them off for yet
more unfinished business, but focus, instead, on the heart that
loves as is. This means completing one life before we start another, taking one evolutionary leap at a time.

This suggestion to reflect on the possibilities of work to be
completed and hearts to be touched is no lazy fantasy. Many
readers of this book may not have another year. *You* might not
even have another year. Only our incessant denial and wishful
thinking assure us otherwise. In my experience, a year before
they died, even those with advanced cancer and AIDS (and
their physicians) did not believe that they had only a year to
live. Even the men I worked with on death row in San Quentin
in the seventies, who had been given a date of execution and
were better informed than almost anyone as to the time of their
death, still displayed a denial of death as intense as that on
Wall Street. One fellow, who had eaten his "last meal" three
times in the holding cell next to the gas chamber before he re-

ceived a stay of execution, spoke of marveling at how the mind repeatedly fantasized about what it would do and say in the days to come.

Of course, the reason that some part of us denies that it will die is because it never does. Even Freud, who believed that a sense of immortality was just a delusion of the sub-, or under-, consciousness which he noted had no concept for its own death, missed the point that perhaps the reason something within feels immortal is because it is. Nonetheless, whatever denial that-in-us-which-never-dies supports, must be closely examined so that it breeds confidence instead of stagnation.

Few I met have actually had a "last year." Most had only a "last" month or two, a few weeks or days, or a few seconds. To have a whole year to examine one's life consciously in the context of approaching death is almost unique in the human experience. And it gives a person the power to heal that which remains unloved and unloving. But why wait for a terminal diagnosis before opening to the potential grace and wonder of this living moment. No one can afford to put this work off any longer, because almost no one knows the day on which the last year begins.

DYING FROM
THE COMMON
COLD

An interesting way to practice dying is by opening to illness. Each time you get a cold or the flu use it as an opportunity to soften around the unpleasant and investigate how resistance turns pain into suffering, the unpleasant into the unbearable. Notice how discomfort attracts grief. Watch the shadows gather in the aching body. Hear them mutter in complaint and self-pity.

Pity arises from meeting pain with fear. Compassion comes when you meet it with love. When we attempt to escape from our pain we feel a sense of helplessness. When we open to sensations at the very point of their origin, softening into an awareness that embraces, rather than disclaims, its momentary inheritance, we experience compassion and even gratitude (more perhaps for the softening than the need it responded to).

Every time you are ill or have a headache, instead of turning on every appliance in the house to distract yourself, settle into the moment as it is and soften around the discomfort. We have been conditioned to withdraw our awareness from the unpleasant. Break that imprinting! Whatever limits the entrance of awareness limits healing. Allow awareness to go where it may never have been before. Let it enter directly into the field of sensation radiating from the discomfort. Soften and explore the constant state of change within the sensations. Do they move or remain stationary? Do they have a shape? Does the shape remain constant or is that also constantly changing? Watch the unfolding of sensation as a process. If you bang your elbow, notice how that first moment of pain spirals out into space like a skyrocket, then fizzles and falls to earth as a few dull sparks. Let it float. Send loving kindness into the elbow. Don't be embarrassed to have this much love for some part of yourself.

When we begin to respond to discomfort instead of reacting to it, an enormous change occurs. We begin to experience it not as just "our" pain but as "the" pain. And it becomes accessible to a level of compassion perhaps previously unknown. When it's "the" cancer instead of "my" cancer I can relate to others with the same difficulty, and I can send compassion into the cancer rather than helplessly avoiding it and turning its pain to suffering.

As this "experiencing of the personal in its universal aspect" develops, we feel a great weight lifted in what can now be seen as "the" mind. When it's "my" depression, "my" cancer, "my" AIDS, I am isolated from the source of my greatest comfort. I am locked in with my suffering and unable to give it any succor. But when it's "the" depression, I take it less personally and am not too threatened to investigate it. When it's "my" unworthiness I feel unworthy to explore it. But when it's "the" unworthiness—the pain that so many struggle with—compassion flows naturally toward it. It is said that we must love ourselves before we can love anyone else, and this is true. But the opposite is equally true: We must love others before we can love ourselves, before we can even recognize ourselves. Seeing the universality of our shared condition offers a broader path of healing on which to continue.

The day I realized it wasn't my mind or my pain, but just the nature of the mind and pain itself, was an initiation that changed my relationship to pain forever. When it's "the" pain, it has the whole universe to float in; when it's "my" pain, I'm standing alone in it.

Open yourself to discomfort. Meet it with mercy, not fear. Recognize that when our pain most calls for our embrace, we are often the least present. Soften, enter, and explore, and continue softening to make room for your life.

The next time you have a cold, practice dying. And in the spaciousness of surrender watch the fear of death bound through with its attendant scenarios. Take each breath as though it might be the last. Watch your life pass before your eyes. Did you notice something left undone? Do it on the next clear day. Practice living.

RENEWING

EVOLUTION

There are two main elements that constitute the foundation for this life renewal. If they are not in balance, not equally cultivated, evolution becomes much more difficult than it needs to be.

The first element is the exploration of what has gone before as a way of clearing a path for what is to come. The central technique for this is the life review that can take months of gradual reflection on the triumphs and disappointments of one's past, and committing to a practice of forgiveness and gratitude. The life review goes beneath the surface of past action to the states of mind from which these acts originated. It examines the emotional attachment to the shadows these previous actions cast in the present. This process of looking back needs to be accomplished with very soft eyes and an accepting heart. If we look back with hard eyes, judgmental and unforgiving, almost no one can stand the view. A much revered teacher once said that if his students were going to thank him for their good fortune then they had to thank him for what they considered misfortunes as well. It reminded me of the

breadth of the work to be done. It became the midnight sun by
which I navigated when the mind had forgotten but the heart
wished to go farther.

As will be explained in detail later, to aid the life review and
bring us more completely into the present, we need to keep a
journal in which we record (and share after your death) the
bright days of inquiry and insight as well as the dark nights of
the soul. This is a journal of states of mind and levels of being.
It makes good reading when the going gets tough. It displays
how every moment of anger, fear, and posturing has been a
moment of grief—a reaction rather than a response to loss—
and that no state no matter how dark or oppressive is new. Although each afflictive emotional state insists it is never going
to go away and will only get worse, this is not what happens.
There is a hallucinatory quality to heavy states that causes us to
doubt our capacities and power. That doubt is as valuable an
exploration for the mind as it is for the heart. It takes confidence to watch doubt without thinking we have to do something about it, trusting its natural impermanence to carry it
away as long as we don't pull back from it or compulsively
react. It is important to become familiar with doubt sufficiently
to be able to turn toward it instead of away.

The second aspect of the yearlong experiment is to become
more present, more mindful of the process we call our life, cul-
tivating a soft-belly practice as a means of opening to the
moment, without clinging or resistance. When developed in
tandem with a mindfulness/insight practice, gradually opening
depths of consciousness are experienced in a daily investigation of the heart and mind.

Just as the first aspect of the work brings our life into the
present, the second aspect explores this "present" as the mo-

ment-to-moment unfolding of the "passing show" of consciousness. We come to know our states of mind intimately, watching
our long-conditioned patterns from an open and compassion-
ate awareness that neither clings to nor condemns the evolving
process.

These exercises in deepening awareness, in broadening forgiveness and gratitude, increase the vigor and sensitivity of
even our most ordinary day. This sense of being more fully
alive further encourages an exploration of our attitudes toward
death, and an investigation of our somewhat submerged, often
contradictory, belief systems. It produces a deep sense of peace
and a particular confidence when it reflects on the potential of
a conscious death. When the life review is well under way and
some daily increase in awareness, no matter how slight, is observed, the two essential elements of our evolution begin to
potentiate and reinforce each other: The "psychological work"
of the life review and the "spiritual work" of a focused awareness combine to create a greater sense of balance and ease.
Without this openness of the "psychological," and depth of the
"spiritual," we are unable to integrate even our most beneficial
insights and enlightenments. They will remain only what we
know and seldom what we are.

Each level requires equal inquiry and observation. When
one level is fostered to the detriment of the other we develop a
psychological limp or a spiritual swagger.

As simple as all this may sound, it is not so easy. It takes
work to place both feet firmly on the ground and become a
whole human being.

Thirty years ago I got lost while hiking in the Sonora
Desert of southern Arizona with a Zen friend from Japan.
Though we were only a few miles from the wildlife sanctuary I

was tending for the Nature Conservancy, I realized, as sunset began to fade into evening, that we might need to spend the night out in the desert. In an effort not to frighten or upset my friend, I told him it might take us a bit longer to get back than we had originally supposed. Recognizing that my very attempt to assure him was itself a product of fear he smiled and said, "It's okay, survival is highly overrated." I recall thinking at the time, "How many deaths, how many previous incarnations does one have to remember before this becomes one's genuine attitude toward death?"

Over these last decades working with the terminally ill, coming to see a bit beyond death and the fear of dying, as in the one-year experiment, there arises a sense that only this moment has any reality and all else, including the very instant passed, is a dream that, if unmindfully dreamt, obscures our true nature.

And the answer to that question of thirty years ago becomes obvious: You have to remember only one life, one death—this one! To enter fully the day, the hour, the moment whether it appears as life or death, whether we catch it on the inbreath or outbreath, requires only a moment, this moment! And along with it all the mindfulness we can muster, and each stage of our ongoing birth, and the confident joy of our inherent luminosity.

When our son Noah was working as a medical technician in a Santa Cruz hospital, he was the fellow who administered the AIDS tests and, two weeks later, pronounced the results. He saw part of his job as reminding patients that while waiting two weeks to hear whether you have a fatal degenerative disease can put strain on the mind, it was also an opportunity for the heart, for insight and reflection on priorities, goals, and desires. He suggested a mini "moment-to-live" practice, recommending to each person that, during the sometimes interminable waiting period, they closely watch how their mind related to either possible outcome. To note the full range of the emotional roller coaster, and to remember that they were not the only ones going through this ordeal at this time, to sense the community of beings holding their breath in case it might be their last. He asked them to remember that it was not just *their* mind that seemed to be going crazy at times, but *the* mind. Big surprise! The survival engineer has hit the panic button! He recommended they ask themselves two questions, first: If you receive a positive diagnosis, what will you do next, who would you share this disturbing news with, and what changes might you make in your life? The second question was: If you find you don't have the AIDS virus, that you have a second chance so to speak, what will you do with your life?

What if they don't discover an escape clause in their contracts? What if they have to go on living? What changes in their lives might make this easier if they had to go through it again? Or if it was actually time to prepare to die? After each of the more than three hundred negative "you don't got it" diagnoses (he said he never had to tell anyone they had the disease), he would remind them that if they had imagined during the two-week reflection that they might "get serious" if given a fatal prognosis, or "get a bit looser" from a clean bill of health, or vice versa, what were they waiting for?

Turning to Ondrea and me before he left for Asia a few months ago, Noah said, "Once you see what the heart really needs, it doesn't matter if you're going to live or die, the work is always the same."

FAMOUS LAST

WORDS

Too many bad movies have left us with a penchant for fantasizing our own famous last words. The mind goes for that sort of thing, like Narcissus for the pool. In that secret cache of personal melodrama where we rehearse so many worlds, we have come to a hundred heroic ends. We have whispered, just loud enough for all those gathered around the bed to hear, magnificent salutations, witty repartee, and poetic conclusions. But what words would you actually utter as you expelled your last breath?

I have seen many die, surrounded by loved ones, and their last words were "I love you." There were some who could no longer speak yet with their eyes and soft smile left behind that same healing message. I have been in rooms where those who were dying made it feel like sacred ground.

I have also been with those who could not die in peace or found some deeper truth only as the light in the body diminished, leaving so much left unsaid and incomplete. I have seen some die blessing all around, and others begging everyone's forgiveness. Although the latter might not seem a "preferable death" for the person who previously found it impossible to address unfinished business, it was an important evolutionary step, a breakthrough access to the heart. It was, as one widow put it, "a very late beginning." Some don't catch up with their life until a few days, hours, or seconds before their death. Others decide to avoid the "last-minute rush" and begin now. Those who have more time discover that this "catching up with oneself" is the first awkward stage of their ultimate completion. Those who do not, find this the painfully uneven ground from which they must depart. Indeed, this stage of growth, of looking ourselves squarely in the eye and recognizing the work still necessary to become whole, the hearts to be touched, the amends to be made, and the thank-you cards to be sent, is painful and life-expanding for everyone. But some have more time and opportunity to integrate these insights, and act on them.

Once again the teaching is clear, prepare now for death so as to intensify and fulfill your life. Don't imagine your endorphins are going to do it for you "when the time comes." When the time actually comes, what is found then will be what is found now.

There is no way to predict what will occur on one's deathbed except to recognize that the mind tends to follow its usual patterns. As Ondrea says, "We die the way we live."

The single most mitigating factor seems to be that those who have had some time to prepare for death, perhaps through long illness, being with others who died, or genuine spiritual practice, seem less concerned with heroics than clarity and compassion. They do not require the orchestra to play their theme as they exit, although several have mentioned almost ecstatically that they could hear it tuning up.

I remember a fellow who discovered during a routine medical exam that he had a very advanced cancer. He said that the
chief cause of his anger was the complete lack of preparation
for dying he had received during his life. He said it took him
thirty-five years to learn how to live and now he had only a few
months to learn how to die. He was pissed. But he caught his
breath and focused on his life. Opening to his rapidly changing
present over the next few months, he found some peace. His
last words, spoken into the air as if to an invisible presence,
were, "Okay, okay."

But what if death is sudden? What if we don't see it coming?
Can we still die in peace? Have we healed our disappointments? Have we met our pain with kindness and awareness instead of continuing to ostracize it and send aversion and even
hatred into it? Have we learned by meeting our pain with
mercy instead of fear how to keep our hearts open in adversity?

If you were driving on a highway tomorrow listening to
your commuter-type thoughts on the way home and all of a
sudden the car beside you had a blowout and swerved into
your vehicle and you felt your car being crushed, what famous
last words might be elicited? I suspect it might be the Great
American Death Mantra: "Oh, shit!" Which are probably the
most often spoken last words of those who die in accidents.
On the autobahn it's *"Scheiss!"* in Paris it's *"merde!"*

Last words are as spontaneous as the life that produces
them. If we speak now with care and consideration, if we use
our words now to express our heart, that is the voice that will
speak for us as our awareness gathers to depart.

7

FEAR OF FEAR

We say we are afraid of death, but what exactly does that mean? Well, first and foremost, that fear seems to represent all fears. It's the leader of the pack. It says, Don't hurt me.

Clearly, all fear has an element of resistance and a leaning away from the moment. Its dynamic is not unlike that of strong desire except that fear leans backward into the last safe moment while desire leans forward toward the next possibility of satisfaction. Each lacks presence. Each is a form of attachment whether "positive," grasping, or "negative," pushing away. Both this clinging and condemning ensnare us in a flight-or-fight relationship to the object of awareness that produces these states of consciousness. When the object floating in our consciousness is a hot fudge sundae, our attention is drawn toward it by desire and we attempt to materialize it at our local Baskin Robbins. When the idea hovering before us is death, we attempt to withdraw our attention, to turn away from it so it can't catch up with us, to dematerialize it at our local church, synagogue,

brothel, or McDonald's, whatever makes us feel the most solid
and undying.

We say it is death that causes all this fear, but it's really
caused by our attachment (positive or negative, as excitement
or dread) to past fears. Especially in times of stress, we tend to
follow well-worn paths and patterns. Our unwillingness to
enter each moment fully, without judgment or the need to control it, simply produces more fear and resistance to that fear.
We need to explore the moment in its unfolding, noting its
preferences and patterning, its process and dynamics. We need
to watch thwarted desire become first frustration, then resistance, then a kind of dishonored pride (hurt feelings) and the
nausea of helplessness, and soon aggression, doubt, and a trembling avoidance of these feelings of dissonance and imbalance.
We feel smaller and less safe with each tightening around the
object of our fear. Scrambling for some means of escape from
such afflictive states of mind, even death at times may seem
preferable to the fear of death.

In the gymnasium of life, the states of mind around death
are a three-hundred-pound weight. Even if you and I attempted
with all our might to lift even a few hundred pounds together,
we would probably be unsuccessful and become resistant to
any further kind of weightlifting. But you and I can work out all
day with the five-, ten-, and even twenty-pound weights, gradually building our strength. We miss our daily opportunity to
increase our stamina by overlooking those little workouts life
constantly makes available—the little fears and doubts, the
slight angers, the five- and ten-pound weights of an ordinary
day that we do our best to ignore, burying that which might
set us free. These lesser pronouncements of heavy states can be
accessed, entered, and investigated with some ease without

their intensity clouding our awareness. Through exploring these often suppressed feelings that we are so proud we can "handle," our insight and letting go begins. There is nothing to fear in fear. Enter it. Begin to relate *to* it rather than solely *from* it. Do not fear fear, soften that compulsive resistance. Fear of fear is ignorance of fear.

Of course, fear creates dissonance in the body and mind, but don't withdraw your attention. Stay with it, watch this state of mind that seems so personal display its quite impersonal dynamic. Even the fear that sustains the judging mind doesn't know you from the person next to you. When Jesus suggested we not judge others, he knew it would free the judging mind from self-mutilation as well. He knew that once you get that juggernaut of judgment rolling, it will flatten you.

In our fear of death, what calls out first for examination is not death but fear itself. We need to explore this hardness in the belly that is so much a part of the armoring over the heart. There is a technique that is ideal for working with fear and letting go of holding. It is soft-belly meditation, an "opening practice" that dissolves resistance and increases the spaciousness in which the investigation continues. Don't let its simplicity dissuade you from plumbing its depths. As soft-belly meditation develops into a soft-belly practice, it offers us further access to subtle blockages, and eventually breakthroughs, to our original spaciousness.

This primary opening practice of soft-belly begins the letting go of a lifetime of holding. It makes room in the body and mind for our whole life. As we focus on softening the muscles, the tissue, the flesh of the abdomen, the breath begins to breathe itself in a new openness. In the increasing spaciousness of soft-belly, thoughts float like bubbles. Feelings come and go in a softness that does not tighten around anything that passes through. This expansive awareness observes judging thoughts as simply the next in line to express the suffering we have become so inured to that we don't notice any longer how hard our belly has become.

As a fellow just beginning this practice asked another who was near completion, "If I have only a year in which to soften my belly where do I begin?" "In your heart," said the other.

SOFT-BELLY MEDITATION

Taking a few deep breaths, feel the body you breathe in.
Feel the body expanding and contracting with each breath.
Focus on the rising and falling of the abdomen.
Let awareness receive the beginning, middle, and end
　　　of each inbreath, of each outbreath
　　　expanding and contracting the belly.
Note the constantly changing flow of sensation
　　　in each inhalation, in each exhalation.
And begin to soften all around these sensations.
Let the breath breathe itself in a softening belly.
Soften the belly to receive the breath,
　　　to receive sensation, to experience life in the body.
Soften the muscles that have held the fear for so long.
Soften the tissue, the blood vessels, the flesh.
Letting go of the holding of a lifetime.
Letting go into soft-belly, merciful belly.
Soften the grief, the distrust, the anger
　　　held so hard in the belly.
Levels and levels of softening, levels and levels of letting go.

Moment to moment allow each breath its full expression
   in soft-belly.
Let go of the hardness. Let it float
   in something softer and kinder.
Let thoughts come and let them go,
   floating like bubbles in the spaciousness of soft-belly.
Holding to nothing, softening, softening.
Let the healing in.
Let the pain go.
Have mercy on yourself, soften the belly,
   open the passageway to the heart.
In soft-belly there is room to be born at last,
   and room to die when the moment comes.
In soft-belly is the vast spaciousness in which to heal,
   in which to discover our unbounded nature.
Letting go into the softness,
   fear floats in the gentle vastness we call the heart.
Soft-belly is the practice that accompanies us throughout the day
   and finds us at day's end still alive and well.

Soft-belly is a trigger for our letting go. Softening melts the armoring over the heart, experienced as hardness in the belly. Each time we remember to be present, to be mindful, we soften into the moment. Softening becomes a call to the heart that it's safe to be alive in the body once again. Soft-belly brings an end to our fear of fear.

8

NOTICING

An essential element of both mindfulness and life-completion practices is the technique of noting, the recognition and defining of our states of mind. Noting is the foundation of the progression through the steps of the life review and journaling practices that make up one arm of this exercise. It is also a basic technique for becoming more present.

Our life is composed of events and states of mind. How we appraise our life from our deathbed will be predicated not only on what came to us in life but how we lived with it. It will not be simply illness or health, riches or poverty, good luck or bad, which ultimately define whether we believe we have had a good life or not, but the quality of our relationship to these situations: the attittudes of our states of mind.

What we describe as "our life" is not the sum total of what has passed through our hands but what has passed through our minds. Our life isn't only a collection of people and places, it is a continuum of the ever-changing feelings they engender. As one practitioner said, "Even our past has a life of its own. It isn't only what you've touched, it's what you've felt of what you touched."

To know your life is to know intimately what you are feeling. Or, to put it another way: to be aware of what state of mind predominates in consciousness. This noting of mental states encourages a deeper recognition of what is happening while it is happening. It allows us to be more fully alive to the present rather than living our life as an afterthought. It enables us to watch with mercy, if not humor, the uninvited swirl of "mixed emotions" not as something in need of judgment but as a work in progress.

The mind is in a constant state of flux. No thought, no feeling, no sensation lasts for more than an instant before it is transformed into the next state, the next thought, the next sensation. Our life lasts only a moment. Note those moments. Acknowledge to yourself, silently in the heart, the various states passing through. Call them by name. Note "fear," note "doubt," note "compassion" as these states pass through. Let this naming of states be a gentle whisper in the heart, not a grasping at conceptual straws in the mind.

Notice anticipation, note doubt or expectation. Watch the process of mind unfold moment by moment, thought by thought, feeling by feeling. As they pass through, note such states as confidence, bewilderment, effort, trust, distrust, pleasure, discomfort, boredom, devotion, inquiry, pride, anger, desire, desire, desire.

This technique becomes refined through practice. To begin with, close your eyes, focus the attention inward, and count how many states of mind come and go in just five minutes. At first we may notice only a dozen or so. But as the method of relating to these states, instead of compulsively reacting to them, develops, they no longer distract us from our observation and they are gradually exposed to inquiry, joining the lineup with all the other suspects.

Eventually, we may notice literally hundreds of subtle changes in those five minutes: qualities of attraction or repulsion meeting every single input from the senses. We seldom see without some sense of liking or disliking, no matter how subtle it is. We open and close from sound to sound, taste to taste, smell to smell, sensation to sensation, thought to thought, and feeling to feeling. We like the way the light strikes one side of the ball but dislike the shadow that it casts.

This constant appraisal gives rise to numerous states of mind, from aversion (ranging from fear, anger, and disappointment to guilt, shame, and hatred) to attraction (including anything from appreciation, gratitude, and the deepest love to lust and greed). Note which states of mind accompany each moment of liking and disliking. What are the states that comprise the feeling of being safe? What states create a feeling of being unsafe? When we say we are happy what are those constituent states? And which states create a feeling of unhappiness or turbulence? When Socrates suggested we should know ourselves, this was the level he was referring to. When we recall the statement "Physician, heal thyself," this is where the healing begins.

It is particularly important to notice this constant liking and disliking that leaves us exhausted at the end of the day. It is from this mechanical response/reaction that our actions and reactions, our karma, arises.

Because noting states of mind as they arise keeps us present, it allows us to meet difficulties at their inception—before they become more real than we are. We note "fear" when the gut tightens in self-defense. We note "mercy" when that state of mind embraces all others. We note "resistance" or "distrust" when we are nodding in agreement but have closed our hearts in self-protection.

The noting of states of mind offers much of the same preparation and recognition as *The Tibetan Book of the Dead* and other afterworld odysseys. In such books, states of mind are personified as angels or demons, bodhisattvas or *asuras*. But an ongoing practice of being present to changing states cuts out the conceptual middleman or -woman, as the case may be. It is a naming of things as they are without embellishment or any need to abstract. It makes approachable those afflictive emotions and heavy states that obscure the heart of our original face. Once we know that we can't let go of anything we don't accept, the noting brings us into the presence of that which so often distracts us from the present. It allows the healing in. And as we observe the appearance of things, we more easily acknowledge their subsequent disappearance, and so come to an appreciation of impermanence.

This practice of self-awareness that began with just five minutes of noting passing states initiates a noting that continues throughout the day. At first we notice not so much what the state is but simply that a change has occurred. Once we can see the major shifts from opened to closed, from liking to disliking, we will be able to acknowledge them before they gain momentum. At this stage we perhaps note fear sooner than kindness. Gradually, as the process of noting becomes more refined, we are able to note subtler and subtler arisings more quickly, until we come to recognize the states before they can even clear their throat to speak by the unique pattern each generates in the body.

It can be hard to die when we have forgotten so often that

we are alive. Noting is a remembering of the present. It creates a living trust.

How many states of mind in five minutes, in five hours, in five days, in five lifetimes? How often has our life passed unnoticed? How soon will we accept this opportunity to be fully alive before we die?

A

COMMITMENT

TO LIFE

What a luxury to have a year to live! With 250,000 people dying each day, and knowing we are somewhere down that line, who has time to put life aside? We prepare for death by living every second, living life minutely, exploring our body and mind with a merciful awareness. To be this close to the moment in which our life is unfolding we need to cultivate a deeper awareness through the development of a meditation practice.

Awareness is itself a healing quality. Where awareness is focused the deepest potentials for clarity and balance present themselves. Though what we are aware of may be incessantly changing, awareness itself remains a constant, a luminous spaciousness without beginning or end, without birth or death. It is the essence of life itself. It is what remains when all that is impermanent falls away. It is the deathless.

I am suggesting living a year so profoundly alive that we di-

rectly experience the moment-to-moment process that is our
lives. We take responsibility for being alive, recognizing that
responsibility is the ability to respond instead of the compul-
sion to react. We explore it all: that in us which at times wishes
to be dead as well as that in us which never dies. That which
blocks the heart and confuses the mind as well as that which
clears confusion and dissolves obstruction.

Not imagining that "death will take care of everything," we
come to realize that our "knowing," even our "understanding,"
is not enough. We must integrate our insights and encourage
the weary mind to settle into the expansive heart. We begin to
live our life firsthand, tasting our food instead of thinking it, listening to the music instead of just humming it, seeing a new
face without characterizing it. We break the dreamlike quality
of a half-attended life. Just as the exploration of awareness begins by remembering we are conscious, so the one-year life exploration begins by remembering we are life itself unfolding as
thought, as feeling, as evolution.

Celebrate each birthday (your own and those of your loved
ones) as though it were the last, remembering that love is the
only gift worth giving. Disappear into each lovemaking as
though it were the first, remembering that your partner is as
frightened and as full of love as you are.

When you speak and when you listen, stay mindful that the
fear which limits greater openness also limits self-awareness
and obstructs the completion of unfinished business. Remember to keep that "other" as the subject of your heart instead of
just an object in your mind.

And in the moments, on the days, in the weeks, when the
mind is so clouded with its own arguments, judgments, and
confusion that there is no real clarity, be compassionately

aware of this too and let it float kindly and unjudged in the vastness of merciful awareness. Let it come and let it go, which means to just let it be in a gentle noninterfering awareness. Note it, but do not judge it. Acknowledge the holding and explore whatever tension or discomfort there is while investigating its process and patterning.

Remember that the ever-present luminosity into which our ever-impermanent density dissolves is the light of awareness by which consciousness is seen, our essential nature which never dies.

This one-year, last-year life experiment is not some morbid undertaking, quite the reverse. It does not invite death but rather encourages completion before dissolution. Although some suicidal niche in the mind might become enamored with the prospect of dying and welcome its demise at the end of the year, such old-mind tendencies invite close examination. They are that part of each of us which would rather die than face, much less heal, our pain. They are the all-too-familiar feelings of powerlessness and inadequacy, which, when they are investigated, remind us of why so many parts of our life remain unlived. The one-year life experiment is a remedy for, not an indulgence of, such life-denying tendencies. In the course of its daily application, life becomes more vibrant and appreciated. It can be vital medicine for so many aspects of ourselves that have become breathless and numb.

Our daily exercise of becoming more fully alive, begun with watching (and, at first, counting) our states of mind, becomes an ongoing practice of "noting" the contents of the mind as they flow through the moment. As one practitioner put it, "We become more present the more present we become."

When this mindfulness practice associates with the cultivation of gratitude and forgiveness, ordinary miracles often present themselves as sudden understandings, insights into the nature of the mind and body, and spontaneous glimpses of our enormity.

Practicing the soft-belly meditation, we make room in our body, mind, and heart for the healing that needs to be done. Once soft-belly has been practiced for fifteen minutes a day for a month or so, we are ready for a mindfulness/insight practice that can make very skillful use of the spaciousness established. Practice soft-belly before the mindfulness of breathing exercise. Focusing one-pointedly on the breath, come back to soft-belly each time you become lost in thinking, returning to the sensations in the breath by softening and opening the space in which they can be observed. As we watch the breath, everything that arises in the mind is noted at its inception as thought, sensation, memory, and emotion, momentarily obscuring the clear reception of the living breath, accentuating how difficult it is to remain present, and how easily we lose contact with our life long before we die.

Having written extensively about the practice of mindfulness in *A Gradual Awakening* I suggest that you refine your practice with this book as well as Jack Kornfield's excellent *A Path with Heart.*

We establish a daily practice of twenty minutes at a time. Within a few weeks or months, increase this to forty minutes, then, as the heart suggests, an hour each morning, eventually adding twenty minutes in the evening to unravel the events of the day before we enter the considerable possibilities of a lucid dream life.

When we wake up each morning, we must notice whether

we are taking an inbreath or an outbreath. Neither is preferred; it is the strengthening of awareness that is the goal. To intensify this waking up fully awake, we can add the practice of not moving from the position we find ourselves in, unless motivated by discomfort, as a means of investigating how many of our actions are driven by negative attachment. Even if we fluff our pillows and attempt to find the most comfortable position, we will soon observe that physical, and thus mental, disquiet arises. We feel that if only we could move that leg a few inches over we would be really comfortable. But once we do this we realize that the new position is just as uncomfortable and so we keep trying to adjust our posture to conform with some imaginary concept of comfort. If indeed we do find a "sweet spot" we believe that nothing could entice us away, but then we discover that we need to go to the bathroom. If we continue this practice we will watch ourselves being prodded by discomfort to sit on the toilet and then eventually being forced to leave it again. We will notice how we are driven to eat by hunger and moved by social fears and considerations to go to work, until one day we will realize how much of our life is a compulsive attempt to escape discomfort. We are motivated more by an aversion to the unpleasant than by a will toward truth, freedom, or healing. We are constantly attempting to escape our life, to avoid rather than enter our pain, and we wonder why it is so difficult to be fully alive. As Jack Kornfield says of life, as of any other lottery, "You must be present to win!"

Continuing this exploration of our motivations we eat our breakfast mindfully, feeling the fork in our hand, watching the energy of desire, tasting each mouthful, putting the fork down between mouthfuls, attending so closely to this usually automatic, unconscious act that a subtler, deeper level of consciousness begins to draw all such compulsive activities into clearer awareness.

Having committed a year to catching up with our life, establish a daily practice of awakening. There are many remarkable psychological processes and therapies, but nothing will do for you what a meditation practice can. No other healing will reach quite so deeply. When the mind has softened its belly and let go of the hardness that obscures our inherent clarity, our senses open in a most gratifying manner. We can hear more subtly, see more detail, and thought becomes more lucid and distinct as our feelings are experienced floating in an expanding awareness. We settle into a moment-to-moment mindfulness of the changing sensations within each breath, watching thoughts arise and disappear, letting go of all that obstructs the vastness of our birthright. Approaching our true nature, like a pilgrim weary from the long journey who can at last put aside his pack, we rest in being.

Committing a year to our own well-being, we live mindfully: eating, working, breathing, even thinking, in greater awareness of our inner processes. We attempt to meditate each morning, to be fully present, no matter how difficult it may seem as that restlessness, which we have so long neglected to examine, begins to stir. Meditation calls all these parts of us back into the heart.

FEAR OF

DYING

We say we are afraid of death, but more likely we are referring to the travails leading up to death: the fear of dying. This in turn is clearly our fear of finding ourselves in a situation over which we have no control, with our reserves exhausted and our body wracked with suffering. This fear, however, is one of the few that can be dealt with materially. The science of pain management has improved radically over the past few years. Now the enormously successful use of an MST Continuum (a continuous infusion of morphine sulfate perfectly adjusted—titrated—to the individual patient's needs; in Canada it is called Voluntary Pain Management) can usually provide an almost painless final round. By titrating the pain medication to the peaks and valleys of the patient's pain, a well-trained physician can adjust the level and frequency of the pain inhibitor to suit the unique needs of the patient in just a few days. This allows people to stay open and awake in those precious final weeks, not dazed or distracted by nightmares produced by too much medication nor feeling defeated, fatigued, and frightened from too little. No longer do patients have to writhe in sweat-soaked sheets enduring as best they can the four hours between pain shots. In the more enlightened medical environments, it is medication upon request. Or better yet, a pain protocol so well developed that the staff knows before the patient when analgesics may be required. Even for those who wisely choose to die at home, a device next to the bed that administers the MST Continuum automatically can make their last days more capable of love and completion. Except in rare cases of nerve involvement, where attempting to adjust the medication to the severe peaks experienced during movement would of necessity knock the person out, an MST Continuum has changed the nature of dying. Dying and abject suffering are no longer always synonymous.

On the other hand, it must be said that to plan for a painless death would be unwise, as there is often some discomfort that attends the shaking loose of the body by the ascending spirit.

Fortunately we don't have to count on only external treatments to soothe the body. We have an enormous capacity to work with discomfort through inner means. Softening the area and focusing awareness into it gradually increases our ability to trust, and to act from our own considerable genius for healing. It opens an intuition as subtle and insightful as the pain requires. It reminds us to be merciful and examine directly that from which we have so long attempted to escape. It does not ostracize that part of the body which is in discomfort but instead invites it into the heart for relief from the resistance that intensifies suffering.

Although I have seen people who opened like exotic flowers on their deathbed seemingly without much preparation, this is not something you can count on. If you examine most of these spontaneous openings you will find that many of these people lived their lives with some degree of awareness and at least a modicum of common courtesy. I have seen even those who have long since abjured God die in grace. In fact, there is nothing more beautiful than an atheist with an open heart. Atheists don't use their dying to bargain for a better seat at the table; indeed, they may not even believe supper is being served. They are not storing up "merit." They just smile because their heart is ripe. They are kind for no particular reason; they just love.

We build such capacities by repeatedly returning to a mindful heart and learning to work with the tugging imbalances of our sluggish resistance. We stop avoiding our pain at any (and every) cost. We get down to what Buddha said was the job we were born for, knowing that letting go of our suffering is the hardest work we will ever do.

An understanding of our reactions to physical pain offers considerable insight into our attitude toward life in general. Pain stimulates our grief. It brings to the surface long suppressed disquietude and unfinished business. But it is easier said than done to let go of the suffering around pain. Pain is a given in life. If you have a body, if you have a mind, there will be pain. However, suffering is a reaction rather than a response to mental and physical discomfort.

If you were hanging a picture in your living room and you accidentally hit your thumb with the hammer, what would be your immediate reaction? Would you sit down a moment with the pain, soften around it, and send a merciful awareness into it? Or would you do what you have so adroitly learned to do: send anger and even hatred into your pain, tighten around it, increase its discomfort and sense of helplessness, and never take it to heart?

If there is a single definition of healing it is to enter with mercy and awareness those pains, mental and physical, from which we have withdrawn in judgment and dismay. Nothing prepares us so completely for death as entering those aspects of our lives that remain unlived.

We need not die defeated by death, feeling a failure, disappointed, constipated with remorse. It is possible to die at peace, mostly without pain, still learning, filled with gratitude.

We occasionally picture our dying as unexpected, even sudden and violent. Or shudder at uninvited images of our flesh worn away by months of suffering, our body a prison from which we long to escape, our mind a maelstrom of confusion and resistance. Fear says we will not be up to our dying, much less death. It insists that we won't be able to let go into death gracefully, that we're going to botch it. But our inherent wisdom knows better. It does not wait. It lets go now into life. It practices its dying by surrendering the luxury of its suffering. It goes beyond itself to become itself.

So we see that our fears of death are reinforced by our fear of a difficult dying. Yet our fear of dying is really more like the fear of falling, while our fear of death is our trepidation of the landing. In death we "fall" upward. Or, as Walt Whitman put it, "We go upward and onward, and death is different than anyone imagines, and luckier!" Dying is the domain of the body. Death is the domain of the heart. Keep dying in its place—the body. Don't let it affect death. Dying is to death as birth is to life. Each is preceded by what seemed the only possible reality, and each is followed by the next remarkable scenario. As one teacher put it, "We fall from grace to grace." Our next moment of grasping, hell; our next instant of letting go, heaven. Dying, like birth, is begun by the body and completed by the heart.

FEAR CONTEMPLATION

When even an inkling of fear arises, acknowledge it. Note it as "fear." If you notice the mind dwelling in it, spinning out its infernal yarn, note this as "fearing."

The difference between fear and fearing is the difference between freedom and bondage. Fear arises uninvited. At times it believes it's protecting you, and occasionally it is. But far more often it is based on imagined tigers, or imagined selves to be devoured. It is a deeply conditioned, automatic reaction to any feelings of being physically or emotionally unsafe.

The more we turn toward it the more familiar with its body and mental patterning we become, and the sooner we can notice even its slightest arousal, perhaps as a ripple of energy just behind the navel, before its first sublingual incantation can be formed.

We meet it at its inception where what seems to be the possibility of choice exists. We observe it in its infancy as we let it float to the surface, display its last prideful gasp, and dissolve as it will, due to its natural impermanence.

The following is a reflection on the qualities and effects of fear. Practice this exploration each time you become aware that fear is arising. The intention is not to suppress fear; quite the opposite, as one must allow the fear to present itself unimpeded in order to investigate it in its natural environment.

Don't pull back from fear.

Soften the belly and gently enter it.

Relate to the fear, not just from it.

Explore the physical and mental patterns that accompany this
          state of mind.

How do you know this state of mind is fear?

What are its attributes?

Define fear's body pattern.

What is happening in the belly, in the anal sphincter,
          in the spine, in the hands, in the toes?

Where is the tongue in the mouth?

Is it curled up against the palate?

Forward toward the teeth? Pushed downward?

Allow the pattern fear imprints in the body
          to emerge slowly like a photo developing in a darkroom.

Let the tensions in the body and the numbness here and there
          display their configuration for closer inspection.

Focus awareness on the changes unfolding in the mind.

Fear is an ever-changing process of grieving.

Note the multiple states of mind
          that comprise this intricate process.

Watch an instant's tremulous inquiry turn to trepidation,
          then to distrust, then to avoidance and doubt.

To helplessness and feelings of inadequacy.

To aggression, and pride, and then to trepidation once again.

Let fear float, and begin to dissolve,
          in the spaciousness of soft-belly.

Let it come and let it go. There is nothing to fear in fear.

The sincere exploration of fear results in a fearlessness which does
          not even wish fear to go away but to become open and free.

FEAR OF
DEATH

Our fear of death is our fear of the uncontrollable unknown. It is the same old fear. It lies in wait behind our eyelids as we awake each morning. It is the fear of fears. It needs space to breathe.

Zen master Suzuki Roshi said that if you put a wild horse in a small stall it can go mad and kick out all the slats, but if you lead this same stallion to an open meadow and let him go, he will run about for a while then settle down, roll in the grass, and go to sleep. Just so with the wild rumors that echo back and forth in the tiny cortex and turn the body to shattered stone. Allowing the fear to float in an awareness that relates *to* it instead of *from* it, we examine the warp and woof of its textures in the body and examine its process in the mind as if it were occurring to our only child.

As awareness embraces fear, control becomes less an issue, and the mind sinks into the heart. There is a space into which we can let go of even the confusion that is reflected from our concepts about death. There is a nonjudgmental softness in which it can float. It is not that the fear goes away completely but that it is less panicked in its own presence. When attempts at control become a prison only letting go of control will result in freedom. When we turn toward our fear of no control, and do not attempt to alter it, our edges become less concrete and we have less to protect.

Imagine what feelings of helplessness and hopelessness might arise if indeed there was no death. Let us not dismiss the fact that though we fear it so, we value it beyond measure. Death makes life safe. Who would sell their death given the opportunity? If you were offered a hundred million dollars for your death, so that you would live 500 years, *no matter what,* who would take the chance? Who would gamble on 350 years in an iron lung, 200 years in a coma, 400 years of Alzheimer's disease? We count on death. Without it we would hardly leave our house, drive 20 miles an hour, stay as small a target as possible, give up all adventurous behavior, watch loved ones suffer interminably, and eventually pray for some release. I sometimes wonder if we would ever have taken birth if we had not been assured beforehand that when it became unbearable we could get out. Death is not the enemy, holding to fear is.

Our fear of the unknown, however, is not as amorphous as we would care to admit. Our fear of death is also our fear of Judgment Day. We are concerned that we may have to account for our actions, that our unfinished business at Karma Savings and Loan may have left us overdrawn or even bankrupt. But as it turns out, there is no Judgment Day, only judgment echoing in the momentary heaven or hell of the mind, scrambling to become acceptable in the eyes of God. We have so little mercy for ourselves and we expect the same from him.

Indeed, we do not know what death will bring. Most people are so unprepared they miss its potential. How many people have you heard about who returned from what is called a near-death experience, having gone toward an amazing light they said was Jesus, Buddha, or the Pearly Gates but never realized that they themselves were that pure light? We are so unprepared for our enormity we project it as something smaller than we are and greater than we judge ourselves to be. Simply to appreciate the light and not merge with it, not to let go into your true self when given the unique opportunities of the dying process, is to miss a grace so profound one might take on another birth just to get it right the next time.

One of those opportunities that death provides is that, as awareness gathers to leave the body, our concentration becomes ten or twenty times what it ordinarily might be. It is this increase in concentration that might explain why so many people, when describing near-death experiences, relate that an enormous peace arose. Concentration has an attendant calm that may contribute to the extraordinary sense of well-being that many speak of at the time of death. Another quality of concentration is its capacity to magnify the contents of consciousness. While making whatever is passing through more obvious and more detailed, it can also make the passing show of consciousness appear more like legitimate theater than the circus that it is. This may explain why afterworlds are described by saint and momentary migrant alike as being more "real and vibrant" than this one. Perhaps it is because they are so much more present, so much more focused.

It may be this extraordinary concentration that in the early stages of death creates tigers from our fear, Buddhas from our piety, angels and devas from our trust, hungry ghosts from our greed, pleasure realms from our sensual longing, bodhisattvas from our compassion, Christs and Mother Marys from our devotion, and giant whistling rectums from our lack of good humor. God and the devil projected from the palpitations of the anxious heart. Or as Krishnamurti said, "The observed is the observer." This is as true in this world as in any other.

Heaven and hell are not places on some metaphysical map, but levels of consciousness we carry with us wherever we go. We create them from our own image and likeness. Heaven is an emanation from the center of the heart. Hell is the heat produced from the friction of opposing desires, a dissonance between what we thought we should be and what we thought we were. It is maintained by judgment and righteous indignation. It is our fallen angel. But the angel ain't dead, she's just in a coma. Soften your belly and breathe mindfully for a while and she will come back to life. All she needs is something more than artificial respiration. The truth will do nicely.

Caring enough for our life to enter it, to explore and heal it, even the hard personal truths that burn are beautiful because they are the truth. As Chögyam Trungpa said, "Meditation is just one insult after another." Although we fear acknowledgment of these holdings may destroy us, they make us invulnerable by displaying the path to freedom. It is exactly this willingness to look into and beyond our suffering that transforms hell into heaven.

Each religion and culture creates its own heaven, terraced like a wedding cake for Buddhists, broad and green as the shimmering Serengeti for bushmen, draped in angel gear, sitting before His wide throne, singing the beatific song that raises Christ and Lazarus alike. Hell is already so familiar, but differs from person to person. For Sartre, hell was "no exit." For Meister Eckhart a hell with Jesus was preferable to a heaven without.

But when all that matters is the deepening of wisdom and compassion for the light and warmth it brings to the eternal moment we share with all that is, we won't even have to pack for the journey. Everything will take care of itself with unexpected grace.

Death is perfectly safe.

THE MOMENT

OF DEATH

There is some disagreement about when death actually occurs. Physicians insist it is when their shiny instruments no longer discern life's presence. They imagine it departs with the last breath. They do not know what happens behind the eyes of the dying. They do not comprehend the inner process continually unfolding. Unable to trust what they cannot measure, they discard death and their deathless essence.

Others say death begins at conception and does not end until that which noisily hurls itself into birth has realized that which remains silently unborn.

Some say the moment of death occurs when the heart stops. But the heart never stops, for when it is no longer contained between opposing ventricles it expands slowly into its inherent vastness without missing a beat, expressing the truth it has embraced for a lifetime.

Others believe the moment of death is when we view the Pearly Gates or meet Buddha waiting for us by the wayside. These, however, are just more of our life experiences in or out of a body.

Death like birth is not an emergency but an emergence. Like a flower opening, it is nearly impossible to tell exactly when the bud starts to become the blossom, or when the seed-laden blossom begins to burst and release its bounty.

Those who know the process directly, from experiences shared with the dying, from decades of meditation, from moments of spontaneous grace, do not speak of death as a single moment before which you are alive and after which you are not. *They refer instead to "a point of remembrance" in which the holding to life transforms into a letting go into death.* It is, just a little way into the process, the moment when something is suddenly remembered that it seems impossible to have forgotten. We "remember" how safe death is, we recall the benefits of being free of the limitations of the body, and ask ourselves somewhat incredulously, "How could I have forgotten something so important, and what was it that made me want to stay in a body?" Death takes on an entirely new context.

At that moment, just before we feel the lightness lifting us from our body, while we are still trying to capture each molecule of oxygen just to stay alive another instant, we suddenly remember we are not the body, never have been, never will be! and all resistance vanishes into a glimpse of our long-migrating spirit. We cut the moorings and dive into the ocean of being, expanding from our body, floating free the mind.

I do not know if this is "the moment of death," but I do know this insight changes everything.

And what is experienced as the point of remembrance leaving the body may function in reverse, on the way back in, as the point of forgetfulness. It is almost as though in order to obtain a body we had to leave on deposit access to some part of our essential wisdom, which can be redeemed upon return of the empty. Perhaps that is why so many speak of never having felt so alive as when they experienced death. Or so dead as when they were in the midst of life.

From this boundless perspective we can appreciate, beyond all worldly reason, how perfect a teaching even death can be, and how immense and intricately woven the miraculous process of our evolution.

THE ACT OF DYING

This is how it is to die:

> *A sense of lightening, an expanding, a floating free.*
> *For some it takes a single seamless sigh,*
>> *for others it is a more gradual ascension.*
> *Either way works. Both astound the heart with unexpected*
>> *joy, both get us where we are going.*
> *But an enormous irony separates the dying from the living—*
>> *a mirror effect in space.*
> *Things are not what they appear.*
> *Each stage of the body shutting down liberates something*
>> *within.*
> *Each outer manifestation of death is accompanied*
>> *by an increasingly expansive aliveness within.*
> *In dying, as in meditation, the deeper we go the less definable*
>> *we become, and the more real we feel.*
> *Immobility is the first outer sign of death,*
>> *but as the element of solidity dissolves*
>> *there is a sense of being unbound*
>> *as pain disappears into a new freedom of movement.*

It's like taking off a shoe that was too tight.
Then the circulatory system closes down, as the fluid
       element withdraws into the departing life force,
        opening within a sense of increasing fluidity.
A feeling of being more like an ocean than a boulder.
The body cools as the fire element converges in the heart
       and exits through the top of the head.
We sense a rising upward,
       like heat radiating from a sunstruck highway.
Lastly, the body becomes rigid and looks more like marble,
       than flesh as the air element disappears into space,
        as the lightness expands into something yet lighter.
Passing beyond dying into death
       a sense of boundless expansion,
       of unlimited possibility,
       continues the inner process.

Dropping our body is like watching an ice cube melt.
We lose our defining shape,
       as we return to our fluid center,
       and evaporate into thin air.
Expanding to fill the room invisible and ever-present.
Like the ice cube we go through enormous external changes
       but our essence remains unaffected.
What once was the ice cube is still absolutely H_2O.
And we are still the immense unnameable.
Dying into death is like that.
Death is another matter altogether.
Anyhow, as Ondrea says,
       Life is the grossest form of being.

14

DYING

CONTEMPLATION

I f you are going to practice dying, the contemplation of death is crucial.

What follows is a meditation used by tens of thousands to prepare for death. It is best undertaken after familiarizing yourself with the description of the dying process in the previous chapter and the comments about the point of remembrance in the chapter before that.

Our story opens with the last breath and closes with the first. It is a thumbnail sketch of an ancient masterpiece. It reproduces some aspects of the process of dying in the same way that an artist's rendering reproduces the Taj Mahal. It's not the real thing, but it's as close as we can get without a passport.

Many people who have had near-death experiences have said that this meditation brought similar feelings, and many reported a deeper trust in the process and a diminished fear of the unknown. One greatly relieved practitioner said, "If dying is anything like that meditation, I don't need to practice dying, I need to practice meditation."

As everyone who has hunkered down for the long haul in

the meditation hall knows, meditation is the practice of the art of dying, of letting go into the vast unknown. Dying meditations redouble this practice.

Read slowly to a friend or silently to yourself, or recorded on tape for repeated listening, this meditation can deepen a sense of letting go. It can open us to the potential of taking our last breath in peace and our next breath in a universe of possibilities and growth. It can open us to the point of remembrance.

PREPARATION TO DIE

OR MEDITATE,

WHICHEVER COMES FIRST

Look about your home for a safe place to die.

Go from room to room surveying the space and sensing if you were to come home to die where that might best be accomplished. Go to that place and just for the work/play of it sit there for this meditation. Later, as the meditation sinks from the mind into the heart and becomes more your own, you will be able to die anywhere.

"Just the simple fact of dying and the fact of the clear light."
—Aldous Huxley

Sit quietly and feel the heaviness, the substantial quality, of the body. Feel gravity pull this dense body toward the ground. Notice the weight of your living corpse. It often wants to lie down. It cannot support its own weight for very long. It is drawn toward the center of the earth.

Notice within this heavy body a flickering field of sensation. A vibratory fluxing full of your relationship to the external world. Feelings of hot and cold, of roughness or smoothness, even of up and down, which have long supported the misconception that we are of the body rather than just in the body. We imagine we own this body but it is ours only on consignment. Notice that the sensations in the heavy body are received by something lighter within. Watch how awareness illuminates each incoming sensation and reports on its existence.

Within the heavy body is a body of awareness, a light body that produces consciousness of the external vessel and the world about it. It is that which experiences life in or out of the body.

Sense the lighter body within. Experience its presence as presence itself. Notice that the sense of being present drifts in a timeless awareness that can never be defined but can always be experienced. Only that which can be named dies, the truth in which it floats has no beginning and no end.

Observe how each breath drawn in through the nostrils of the heavy body is experienced as sensation by the light body within. Notice how each breath connects the heavy body with the light body. Notice how each breath maintains that connection, allowing life to stay one more moment in the body.

Feel the contact between the light body and the dense body that each breath provides. Feel how each breath sustains the light body balanced perfectly within.

Take each breath as though it were the last. Experience each inhalation as though it is not going to be followed by another. Don't try to conserve your breath to stay in the body. Let it come and let it go.

Each breath the last. Let that last exhalation go. And just go on with it.

The last breath of life leaving the body behind. The connection severed between the light body and the heavy body. The end of this life. The final breath.

Don't try to hold on to it, let it go. Let go of your last breath, let the light body float free.

Let yourself die. Let go now. Hold to nothing. Trust the process.

Let yourself die into space. Leave your body behind, follow the light.

The last breath vanished into space. Leave your body where it lies and go on. That was never you. There you are shining before you. Enter that light. It is your own great nature. Do not be frightened by your immensity. Release all that holds you back from your ultimate fulfillment. Dissolve your heart into the great heart. Let who you have always been become who you are.

Gently, gently let yourself float free of the body. Constantly expanding outward through decreasing levels of density into increasing depths of grace. Enter the vastness of being. Rest there in your birthright, your deathright. Accept your inheritance.

Let yourself dissolve into the vastness. Edges melting, boundaries disappearing. Dissolving, dissolving into space. Uniting with the absolute joy of your absolute nature. Space dissolving in space. Light merging with light.

Let go of your knowing, let go of your unknowing, and simply be the presence expanding into the luminosity of its own great heart. Let that which is light follow its well-lit path.

Don't ask the mind for advice, just follow your light. It knows the way by heart.

Let go of your name. Let go of your face. Let go of your reputation and float free in the vastness.

With gratitude and a single sigh leave your body behind with that life you dreamed once.

Notice, as you expand into that sense of safety, that there arises a comfort so deep and natural you wonder where it has been all your life.

Let go of your understanding and float free in your intuition.

Enter the space in which your thoughts are floating. Let go into the light. Light dissolving into light. Space dissolving in space. Consciousness floating free in pure awareness.

Have mercy on yourself. Let yourself go, radiating out into space.

Merging with the Great Heart that has no substance but is as real as you are.

No inside, no outside, just edgeless being in endless space.

Space expanding into space. Light dissolving into light.

Rest in being. Float free in your original spaciousness.

And from the vanishing point on the most distant horizon, watch as something slowly approaches. It is the first breath of life.

And with that breath arrives a new body. Notice in the desires that arise as that new incarnation approaches the dimming of the light that precedes the point of forgetfulness. Attempt to stay alert through the process of reentry.

Each breath the first.

Each breath completely new.

Taking birth once again.

Born back into a body to examine what was born. And what never dies.

Taking birth for the benefit of all sentient beings.

The light body reinhabiting a heavy body. Reanimating life and the possibility of an awareness so clear it obviates any potential for the kind of stillbirth that lasts a lifetime.

Each breath the first.

Born to serve and explore. To deepen the mercy of whatever world we find ourselves in.

Each breath so precious, allowing the light body to remain a moment more within its earthen vessel.

Taking birth into this world to discover the healing we have so long sought. And to sing the song we have been learning since we sat beneath the bo tree or hung from the cross or looked into the eyes of our dying child. No one said it would be easy, only fruitful.

Each breath the first, the last, the only breath available, to carry us beyond our forgetfulness into the scintillating center of the living truth.

May all beings live with death over their left shoulder and kindness in the center of their heart.

May all beings be free of suffering. May all beings know the great good fortune of their great nature.

May all beings be at peace.

JENNIFER

FOR JENNIFER DYING ON HER TWELFTH BIRTHDAY

A cupcake with one pink candle
on the nightstand beside her bed,
Christ crucified on the hospital wall above her.

Most of her youth consumed by leukemia,
her body closing, she let go at last.

And with that last breath
lifted her Jesus from the cross.

The end of years of illness.
Free now to ride her beloved horse.

Sitting beside her empty body,
I sensed ancient Mary, Mother of Mercy,
come to cradle the newly dead in her infinite arms

and the children come slowly to the table
for the supper gently promised at Golgotha.

And I wondered,
all-too-rational and brokenhearted,
how when thousands died that day,
just one Mary could embrace them all.

And offering me her shoulder she whispered,
    When a thousand people look at the moon
    there are a thousand moons.

LIFE REVIEW

It is not uncommon for people who have had a close call with death to say that they saw their whole life pass before their eyes. In a timeless moment faces, conversations, events, sounds, and images from the past were vividly replayed in consciousness. Many people are not completely satisfied with the show. They think that the script could use some work, the plot line left something to be desired, the actors weren't up to their roles, and although at times it seemed boring and too long, the end came too quickly. They are surprised at how much they have forgotten and how much of it there was.

Most immediately fall back asleep into their lives without the recognition that if we don't do something to heal our lives now, someday, when it's more than just a close call and our life flashes by, it will be too late to do anything about it. Let us not wait to review our lives on our deathbed. Consider the possibility of finishing your business before your lease is up.

Once the soft-belly practice is established and the fear contemplation has cleared some space, it is a good time to begin the life review practice to release the past so as to make room for the future.

At nineteen I was thumbing through a book on Buddhism that seemed like an oasis in a desert wilderness, but I felt that I was too impure to be able to make use of it. I believed I had found the answer too late to deal with the load I was already carrying. But I bought it anyway, as an alternative to oblivion. It resulted in a great renewal. From the remarkable bounty that came out of even that faltering willingness to go forward, I can only say, don't allow the mind that is so scared of death, of life, even of its own shadow, to make the decision to clear the future by cleaning up the past. Offer that decision to the heart that has so often been obscured by unfinished business. Offer it the option of finishing farewells, honoring friends and teachers, directing forgiveness to some and asking for it from others.

A primary aspect of the life review is gratitude meditation. It is begun by recalling warm times, old friends, special days, moments of insight and healing, and the love that made it all worthwhile. With gratitude and appreciation we invite each person individually into the heart and open a dialogue with them. Such conversations tend to become quite revealing. After you have shared a real connection, whether it takes several minutes or just a moment, thank them, and as the memory dissolves bid them farewell. Greet each memory with soft-bellied appreciation and part from each reflection by saying good-bye. Each time you leave a memory, pleasant or unpleasant, depart mindfully. There is no assurance you'll ever come that way again even in memory. This simple ritual is not so easy or superficial as you may imagine. Whether made with some sense of loss or with a sigh of relief, our good-byes become more heartful with each departure from the past.

Just as everyone has things to be grateful for, there are events that we may wish had never happened. And they left memories that still seem unresolved, surrounded by, and often associated with states of remorse, guilt, and self-loathing on the one hand, and frustration, anger, and even fantasies of revenge on the other. These painful memories, like any other pain, call out for relief. They are the crux of our unfinished business.

Generally, there are three kinds of memories: pleasant, unpleasant, and neutral. Those that touch our heart are the pleasant memories toward which we direct gratitude. Those that tighten our gut are the unpleasant memories to which we send clarity and forgiveness. Some individuals in our past elicit both responses. The mind may even hold some slight resentment toward those we love. Some whom we feel have hurt us may also have been those with whom we shared special moments and for these we may feel grateful, although our forgiveness practice is tested. The process becomes refined with practice and an openness to unexpected feelings.

The clarity comes from mindfulness of the changing states of mind. The forgiveness comes from a heart that can no longer stand to be closed to itself or anyone else, a heart that values freedom more than it wants to disguise its pain.

Forgiveness finishes unfinished business. It is another primary facet of our life reviewing that should be developed simultaneously with the gratitude meditation. It allows us to move forward and not be held back by an unwillingness to enter our pain as a means of healing it. We allow to come to mind those we feel have hurt us, and speak to them of our feelings, and listen as best we are able to their imagined response. We allow them to apologize if they wish or take flight if they must. We invite them into the anteroom of the heart and, recognizing their considerable pain and confusion, touch them with the possibility of forgiveness just to see how it feels and to sense what healings might be appropriate. There is no rush to this slow and miraculous process. Force just closes the heart. When we have shared a minute or two with that memory and explored and interacted with its contents we bid that person farewell, watching with each meeting and departure the gradual melting of our fear and the reestablishment of confidence in our own process.

As these conversations with our pain continue, we may notice entering from just offstage, as if drawn by the potentials of forgiveness, those people who we wish might forgive us as well. We speak to them and listen very closely to what we feel they might have to say to us in response. We begin finishing conversations and relationships that were left incomplete. We ask for their forgiveness and begin considering what we might do to make things right. It really isn't the act of contrition that sets the mind at rest but the intention not to repeat actions that cause harm.

Just as there are many ways to express gratitude, there are many levels at which we can make amends. Forgiveness meditation offers insight into what might be appropriate. Letters, calls, visits, and, in particular, prayers for another's well-being can be deeply healing. Or take them as the subject of your heart instead of as an object in your mind and join with them playfully in the mystery as you teach them how to forgive and be forgiven. This is no conversation in thin air. Indeed, the atmosphere that separates us has never been more tangible than when we attempt to bridge it. As Nisargadatta said, "The mind creates the abyss and the heart crosses it."

Often the person we wish to make amends to is no longer in our life. He or she may have died, moved away, or disappeared into our remote history. Visualizing conversations enables us to invite, unflinchingly, someone we fear we have hurt into the heart.

A considerable aspect of completing unfinished business is, of course, to repay debts. Some can be repaid with a check; for others we may have to dig deeper. As I moved from the world of shadow to that of light, some forms of my grasping were slower to release than others. At twenty, about a year into my interest in Buddhism, while browsing through an Oriental art store, I pocketed a small nineteenth-century terra-cotta Buddha figure. My stolen Buddha was a scowling, very resolute Bodhidharma who was not about to let me get away with anything. Over the years, though other Buddhas came and went, he was my fiercest teaching in honesty and straightforwardness. Though he never lost his frown, he became a fundamental encouragement to let go of superficial desires and consider the heart. About two years after taking the clay figure I sent a check to the shop with a letter of apology. (I am told that department stores receive thousands of dollars a day from repentant shoplifters.) For a moment I thought I saw old Bodhidharma smile, but then I realized that it was just me. Amends feed the heart and quiet the mind.

Ironically, that fragile, wonderful, scowling, pure love Buddha is one of the only objects that survived these forty years. It sits on our altar beside a gift from the Dalai Lama and the photos of several beloved teachers.

Golden Buddha is wisdom Buddha. Jade Buddha is compassion Buddha. But stolen Buddha is best Buddha of all because it reminds me of the power of renewal.

Before we go further with this very skillful practice I would like to say that I do not believe that a few months of sending gratitude into pleasant memories, and forgiveness into the unpleasant, bidding farewell to the occupants of memory, and being mindful of passing states of mind, is going to remove all the grief from our most painful memories. But it can help long-abandoned feelings find their way back into the heart, where they can be reexperienced in an increasing spaciousness and with a somewhat softer eye.

This does not suggest that we attempt to force forgiveness or gratitude. Simply touching a difficult memory with some slight willingness to heal begins to soften the holding and tension around it. Eventually, perhaps, we will be able to send gratitude into our whole life, not for being wholly pleasant but for being the teaching that brought us to this remarkable moment of introspection.

I cannot speak for anyone else but as I attempted to "get my house in order," inspecting its foundations and my early life in particular, I discovered a youth full of distrust, self-centered gratification, and emotional dishonesty. Often in rereading the early chapters of my life story I discovered no more than a cosmetic concern for anyone else's pain. It was as hard to confront as a three-headed demon on the path. These images were very difficult to confront—they seemed so real and so painful.

But then I remembered that one of my teachers used to say, "The thought of a tiger is not a tiger." The memory of an event is not that event, but its reflection on the constantly changing surface of the mind. These images on the screen of consciousness, some refer to as a kind of gymnasium for the heart, in which we do not attempt to pick up the heaviest weight but to put it down, let it go. Others refer to this stage of relating to the contents of memory-consciousness as being like a rehearsal, an opportunity to work with the feelings attending such situations should they confront us again—say, on the journey through death. It was clear that if I could not open to certain difficult memories now with some compassion and clarity, they would continue to narrow the path through life and death. It is the fear that makes death seem like a shallow pool viewed from a high cliff.

Reviewing our life story, with an intention to both honor and heal the past, can take a few weeks, a few months, or the rest of our lives, as unseen levels of holding gradually arise into awareness and present themselves for recuperation. It is strong medicine, a little bitter at first, but it gets sweeter as forgiveness and gratitude, mindfulness and mercy, make our blessings too many to count. When the forgiveness takes on a life of its own and the suffering has subsided around painful events sufficiently for us to comprehend what they have to teach us, then the past takes on a different meaning. We receive, as Ondrea says, "the gift within the wound," the insight and strength, the appreciation of compassion and awareness, that we need to heal so many other parts of us.

In her book *How to Grow a White Lotus*, Zen master Kennett-Roshi speaks of reviewing her life—incident by incident, insight by insight, in all its triumphs and defeats— after she was informed that she was going to die. She said it brought her squarely into her life. Indeed, the power of her life reflections were so great (and this is not anything I am in any way suggesting will happen for anyone else), her body did not in fact die but continued to house her process toward enlightenment. Although this process was not undertaken as a means of produc-

ing a cure, she found it reassuring that entering into even difficult memories did not prevent one.

Those people who have meditated for a few years probably
have done quite a bit of this work already. Life repeatedly presents itself for review in the 2 A.M. silence of the meditation
hall. Memories arise, feelings are felt, awareness is explored,
the heart accepts, and the next moment comes. When I began
meditating, I could remember very little before the age of nine
or ten. Now I can recall clearly early birthday parties and the
dancing bears' decal at the foot of my crib.

The life review is a matter of focused reflection. We look
back at our life, not as if we still owned it but as though we
were about to give it up. A recollection of the past as though
this might be the last sip of that old wine, the last kiss from that
departed lover, the last time to appreciate a life so full of our
very human experience. It is a healing contemplation.

This process is one of meeting the good times with distinct
gratitude. And the bad times, after the anger has been thoroughly explored in the same way that we might contemplate
fear, with increasing forgiveness. We recognize that bad times
can offer good teachings and open us to deeper ways of living
that produce more happiness than discontent.

Or, as one friend well into this process said, "It's all shit and
sunshine in the beginning, and then it gets worse, and then it
gets better, much better; in fact, there are more and more times
when it all seems absolutely perfect."

In many ways, a life review is not so much a contemplation
of events gone by as it is an inventory of residual feelings—a
recognition of work completed and healings yet to be accomplished.

As one hospice physician said, and several spiritual teachers have noted, "Sometimes the initial breakthrough doesn't result in peace or a healing into anything. Indeed, sometimes people look and feel worse. But they are fuller. They have allowed suppressed and abandoned parts of themselves to surface and finally be served."

A few therapists with whom we discussed the life review were concerned that it might be too difficult for people. They felt that most people's lives had been so hard that they might be better off "not opening that can of worms."

We have certainly taken their counsel to heart and advised those embarking on this process to take it slow and easy. Don't rush over to the heaviest memories and herniate yourself with anger and guilt. Build a foundation of gratitude and mindfulness before exploring the possibilities of offering and requesting forgiveness. Begin with the all-too-numerous resentments and complaints. Let us explore the ache in our heart, and the cultivation of compassion for not only *our* pain, but *the* pain we all share.

In the life review we experience the full range of emotion: outrage at the burdens others have put on us, shame at the burdens we have put on others, gratitude at the gifts received, and joy at the gifts given.

If there has been trauma or abuse it is best not to force such memories. There is plenty to do elsewhere in memory while these thoughts and feelings observe whether it is safe enough to arise.

Indeed, wherever we feel victimized, this may be a difficult exploration because it promises at some level to put us back in the presence of the victimizer, if only in memory. And for that within us which may have victimized others, it feels hellish! But why wait for that either? Why not explore now how we might be "in arrears" and sense what can be done about it. Like the man said, it ain't over till it's over; and until our heart is fully open it will never be over, and we will repeat our infernal holding eternally.

If you are already in therapy, consult with your therapist to see how this practice might affect the present course of your work together. If you are not in a therapeutic relationship with a professional, you might establish a we-can-talk-about-anything relationship with a close friend so as to be able to reflect aloud on your inner process.

There are moments in the life review for all of us when the going gets so tough we have to keep remembering to come back to the heart the way a mountain climber returns to an oxygen mask. Without the process of meeting remembrance after remembrance with soft-belly, forgiveness, and gratitude, the life review can be more arduous and less healing than its potential denotes. It's not meant to be a process of rehashing old thoughts and feelings by the rather dull, somewhat depressed, light of old mind. Rather, it is a regathering of awareness (before death does it for us) to illuminate the past with a new mercy.

Because, as mentioned earlier, the fear of death can include a fear of punishment, the life review can dispel much of this fear by allowing us to take Judgment Day at our own pace. As we work to let go of self-judgment, and offer that part of our suffering to the heart of our desire to be free, there can arise something that seems too good to be true. It is a sense of all-pervading love for ourselves; some say it is like seeing oneself through God's eyes. And the fear of Jehovah diminishes. The elation comes from the approach of the truth itself. The truth that Buddha stated when he said you could look the whole world over and never find anyone more deserving of love than yourself.

When I was working with my life review I looked back at some of the things I had done and I was appalled and ashamed. I wondered whether such ugly footprints would eternally mar the tracks I had left behind and sighed at how difficult I must have made the path for those who had traveled beside me. But confessional breast-beating is of little avail.

We would like to atone for our sins, but it's hard to get a hair shirt nowadays that doesn't have a slogan on it. Then something wiser than our pain reminds us that if we allow ourselves to feel the pain of those we hurt, and send to them wave after wave of intentions for their well-being, there is a healing shared by each person.

Letting ourselves be forgiven is one of the most difficult healings we will undertake. And one of the most fruitful. But as my dear friend Elisabeth Kübler-Ross says, "Nothing is too good to be true."

Recollections arise spontaneously from the underdream, auditioning for our attention. They stand in line waiting to be healed and they ask, What can I do to be at peace with myself so that I may die peacefully? This is a "path-sweeping practice" performed with the intention of healing old wounds and praising old loves. It takes time and is best not delayed until your body strength is dwindling, your concentration weakened, and your emotions distracted by death's approach.

As one fellow said, memory is more like a painting than a photograph. And some of those paintings are a little abstract. Their styles range from Fra Angelico to Picasso. Some have cracked and faded with age. Their outlines have become vague and restless, never quite taking form long enough to be appraised. Even the best intentions at retrieval and completion of such events and feelings may be thwarted.

When I reflected on certain chapters in my story, the details swam in an ocean of competing imagery and attitudes. It was difficult to know what the appropriate response might be. When this happened I simply sent sincere wishes of well-being to those with whom I shared a nearly forgotten moment, asked forgiveness for whatever difficulty my ignorance might have caused, and offered gratitude for the time shared.

There are two other levels at which the life review can be used. The first is called "awakening in the dream," the second is the level at which the life review can be used as one might *The Tibetan Book of the Dead.*

Part of truly preparing for death is the eventual letting go of our story line and looking back on life with equanimity and a sense of completion. We may even wonder, as we watch the pictures on our old screen, Whose life was that anyhow? We watch our lives pass before our eyes as if they were someone else's parade, blowing a kiss to ourselves as we pass by. Becoming like Lakshman in the *Ramayana,* as he sat beside the river preparing to die, reflecting back on his life, saying, "It's like something I dreamed once, long ago, far away."

Our reaction to the past strongly influences our experience of the present. The life review offers benefits that lie not only in appreciating our relationship to past events, but to the past itself. Memory is no less an illusion than any other thought. It constantly changes perspectives and is susceptible to influence from surrounding attitudes. We begin to demagnetize the reactionary quality of memory by approaching pleasant and unpleasant alike with an increasingly unconditional mindfulness, more like an enthralled research scientist than a weary court reporter. No longer willing to live our life secondhand, we enter directly the memory-moment and let our heart pour into it. Acknowledging that the past as well as the present is not as tangible as we would like to imagine, we examine the constantly changing mirage of our memories, which at times has the vague, insubstantial quality of a dream within a dream, and experience that things are not what they seem. This insight is called "awakening in the dream." It recognizes how much memory is a function of our self-image and that our self-image is no more substantial than a thought. At this level we begin to observe the memories there before us as being as weightless and insubstantial as the dreamlike "floating world" that so many refer to in the interstice between dying and death. We awake to watch ourselves dream ourselves.

This awakening does not necessarily get us out of the dream, but it does allow us to recognize that we are dreaming. When we recognize this we are ready for the next level. We can begin to reread our book of life, this time without skipping the footnotes, adding dialogue, or pretending that it is nonfiction. We begin to employ techniques similar to those in *The Tibetan Book of the Dead*, which speaks of the obstacles on the path through death, and how our states of mind project images of ghosts and angels in death as in life. As we relate to the passing show of consciousness—and memory in particular—we recognize that the ghost in front of us is the ghost within. We see that to the degree that we can send healing awareness into it now, we will be able to convert it later from a hindrance into an ally, from a roadblock into a milestone.

This is the practice of watching which memories and thoughts ensnare awareness. We see how fear, lust, guilt, and anger seduce consciousness into fantasies. We identify which images in the mind personify certain concepts and points of view. As one fellow said, "Any point of view is too small for the whole truth." These attitudes are the bones that comprise the skeleton we have hung in our closet. They create this world as much as the next. In this world we project them onto others. In the next they are projected back to us. We are frightened of what the mind might do after death because we know the mind has a mind of its own. We untangle the present by unraveling the knots of the past. Remembering that the etymological root of "nostalgia" is "a reminiscent pain," we do not hold on to the past but relieve it of its burden. Not canonizing our childhood in joy or dread, nor lost wandering between acceptance and denial, we release old holdings and allow life to catch up with itself. We meet ourselves on the path and recognize we are a projection of our own conditioning, and going beyond even this understanding, or any other concept we may be attached to, we merge with our deathless being.

THE LIFE REVIEW PROCESS

The life review begins on a Monday and ends some time before we die.

Sit quietly for a while and bring to mind someone from your past whose kindness touched your heart. Envision yourself speaking to that person. Tell them what they have meant to you. Send your gratitude to them as though your hearts were connected. Thank them, and when the conversation ends, bid them farewell. Say good-bye to them as if you might never see them again, even in memory.

Bring to mind, one by one, and without haste, the friends, teachers, parents, ancestors, comrades, lovers, and even pets with whom you feel a kinship, those who have supported the growth of your heart. Tell them how much you appreciate their care and kindness. Send gratitude into their image. When love has filled the space between you and it is time to depart, say good-bye as if you might never be this way again.

Each time you meet those you care for with gratitude and thankfulness the experience changes slightly as the conversation evolves and the parting becomes less a separation than a completion.

As the practice expands to include not just people but moments from the past for which you feel gratitude, focus your recall of those events and draw that moment of beauty into your heart. Thank your lucky stars! When the scene has completely played itself out, say an appreciative good-bye, and for that moment, don't look back.

The life review and the gratitude and forgiveness meditations evolve symbiotically, each supporting and feeding the other. When we have spent some days or weeks practicing gratitude it is time to develop the forgiveness meditation.

Bring to mind someone who caused you pain. Not the worst offender, but someone for whom you feel more a sense of resentment than hatred or rage. Someone whose memory is unpleasant but is not so anger-inducing that you can't soften your belly to their recalled presence. Easy does it. See how far away from their heart that person must have been to treat you that way, how numb and frightened. Just for this moment, as an experiment in healing, touch them with the possibility, no matter how slight, of forgiveness. See how that feels. Notice how the heart longs to be free of its grief. Let it go, open the fist in which this memory is grasped. Let it float a little freer in the possibility of forgiveness. Let it be touched with mercy by that within you which knows in itself such moments of forgetfulness and even cold indifference. There is a humility to forgiveness that serves well the forgiven as well as the forgiver. A crucial step in self-forgiveness is the forgiving of others. The quality of forgiveness expands even to embrace our "unworthy selves." It is a remarkable process for which we can be grateful.

Gradually, as the mind invites even unpleasant memories, deepen the practice of soft-belly. Softening to hard places lets them melt at the edges. In the ever-increasing spaciousness of soft-belly, invite those memories that still seem to carry some pain or feelings of incompleteness one by one, and without haste. Recognizing this other person's fear, forgive them the pain they could not deal with and spilled over onto you. Forgive them their weakness and arrogance. Take them as the object of a forgiveness meditation. When you feel you have gone as far as you can without forcing anything, bid them adieu. Let them go on their way to be visited again with forgiveness in the near future.

As the practice of attending to specific kinds of memory becomes refined, we no longer need to choose beforehand whether we will be working with pleasant or unpleasant memories but can open the gates to the intuitive flow of whatever memory wishes to present itself. As the life review deepens, let pleasant and unpleasant alike audition for your attention as the heart alternates between gratitude and forgiveness. Notice those that wait just offstage to see if it's safe. Explore the personality of each memory competing for your concern. Note the urgency of some and the reluctance of others. Some are bold and others quite shy. Invite them all in for tea.

As subtler memories of every variety arise into an increasingly gracious spaciousness, we become more confident in the process. The process takes on a life of its own. Sensing possibilities, it becomes eager to go farther, eventually becoming capable of opening to our most guarded closedness. Approach difficult memories as you would a great bonfire. Take one step at a time. Sit down and become accustomed to the heat, then stand up and take one more mindful step forward. Then sit once again to adjust to this new perspective. There is no need to jump precipitously into the fire so the ego-hero can die a Viking's death. Such bravado does not cauterize our wounds. It fuses our helplessness and hopelessness into an imposing sense of personal inadequacy. Only the soft slow approach will do if what we wish to achieve is "a fullness in time," a sense of confident completion. In fact, with some additional focus we may be able to put the fire out from here, not by smothering it with our bodies but by taking away its fuel: our attachment to our suffering, our unwillingness to allow ourselves to forgive or be forgiven.

Of course, the life review is more than revisiting hard times. It is also a feast for the heart. It is an opportunity to embrace those whose embrace you always treasured, to continue conversations begun years before that still resonate in your marrow. It is a chance to bow to those who taught you how to bow and to send loving kindness to those who taught you how to love.

It takes a thousand moments of remembering for us to stay open long enough to relate wholeheartedly to our past instead of from it. And to recognize that what you imagined to be unworkable is already in process.

As we watch again and again the story of our life unfolding, the repetition of, and nonresistance to, the passing show allows us to see it in a slightly less subjective manner. We start to take our life less personally. We watch it as Lakshman said, like something we dreamed once, long ago and far away. Ironically, our life seems less sure than we had imagined, as it becomes a more perfect teaching than we had presumed.

When we project before us a world in our own image and likeness, it is called "small dreaming." It is considered small not only because it encompasses very little of our enormity but because it tends to keep us that way through life as well as death. When we sense there is something in us greater than even our sacred emptiness can describe, first our body, then our mind, and soon our heart, dissolve into a clarity and vastness for which even the word God would be insufficient. We experience the indescribable peace that arises from the heart of the unnameable truth. This is the big dream in which we awake to the nature of our sleepiness, and know *that our life is not defined by its experiences but by the heart that receives them.*

Total recall would be necessary for a full life review, but that might take the rest of one's life. Rather than putting our life on "rewind" and forcing memories, just allow them to arise from the underdream. Gradually withdraw "the censor band" between the known and the unknown, between what has been so awkwardly labeled as the "conscious" and "subconscious" mind. It is ironic that what is called the "conscious mind" is usually subattentive, while the deeper levels, in which the greater part of consciousness and our lives reside, is seen as somehow "subconscious."

We make peace with our lives one image at a time. We stop living as though life was a Shakespearian melodrama we are watching from the balcony, keeping a safe distance, more audience than participant. We do not wait for death to jump on stage, turn to us, and call us by our true name to begin meeting our life scene by scene, act by act, in the bright light of a new day.

The life review makes us recognize how much we have become the casual observers of our lives. We are seldom fully present and are more likely to be thinking our lives than living them directly. We rarely trust letting go sufficiently to become one with our experience. Our distrust of death is directly proportionate to our distrust of life.

Until we stop defining ourselves by memory we will never find out who we really are, or who we really aren't. Indeed, one meditation teacher said that we watch the mind so as to see that the mind is not who we really are, and that what we have been looking for is what is looking. We are awareness itself not limited to the tiny memories and thoughts which arise in that vastness. It is our identification with these thought-molecules that shrinks our enormity to fit our discontent. It increases our fear of being found unworthy of heaven. If we hold on to this fear we experience hell, but if we release it we find ourselves in heaven. Anything that can float can take you to the Other Shore.

When, in previous writings, I have used the term *the Other Shore*, some people have mistaken this to mean death, but, as in classical Buddhist scripture, it refers to complete freedom, such as "enlightenment." Herein lies the rub for so many. We imagine that death is going to do our work for us and set us free. It will not. This is the work we are called on to accomplish ourselves. Death will free us from the body, but we will have to walk the rest of the way on our own.

So let us put down our baggage and die now to the tedious dilemmas of self-loathing and self-aggrandizement. Let us thank our lovers and friends, bow to our teachers, and embrace our trembling fears.

Take a breath directly into the heart, the first breath, the breath of a new life unimpeded by the last.

The pure and simple heart of the Vietnamese Buddhist master Thich Nhat Hanh shines through in the pages of his book, Being Peace. *Thich Nhat Hanh cultivated mindfulness, forgiveness, and gratitude as a powerful remedy in the midst of his war-ravaged country, and his book is a wonderful companion during the life review.*

FORGIVENESS

Forgiveness renews life by finishing unfinished business. Even an unsuccessful attempt at forgiveness has the considerable power of its intention. We cannot force forgiveness because force closes the heart, but we can explore its possibilities, its capacity to heal the forgiver, and sometimes the forgiven.

We may insist that we are not in pain, but that is a measure of how numb we have become, and how much we have had to harden the belly to armor against our grief. This armoring is the "second skin" we have grown, devoid of nerve ends, impenetrable, which lets nothing in and nothing out. But death is a gentle kick in the ass if we can still feel it. It reminds us to forgive now before it's too late to say "I forgive you" or free ourselves from self-recrimination.

Forgiveness does not condone unkind actions, but it does embrace the momentary actor whose unskillful ways led to such unskillful conduct. It does not condone thievery, but simply addresses the broken heart of the thief. It is mercy in action in the same way that compassion is wisdom in action.

FORGIVENESS MEDITATION

The meditative aspect of the forgiveness process is begun by sitting down quietly and bringing to mind someone toward whom you feel resentment. Starting, if possible, with the least transgressor, and very gradually, almost experimentally, expanding that mercy to include all those whose time has come for forgiveness. Some, representing greater pains, may remain outside that circle for a while, or just put one foot in until you tell them otherwise. It is a slow miraculous process.

In this experiment in freedom say to each person "I forgive you." And watch closely for that tightening in the belly. Soften. In your heart repeat silently, "I forgive you." Notice how the mind begins to awaken to possibilities. Speak to that person, tell him or her how you feel. And listen to what your heart has to say.

Say to them, in whatever words are right for you, "I forgive you for whatever pain you may have caused me, intentionally or unintentionally, through your forgetfulness, confusion, anger, distrust, or bland indifference." Tell them in your own words, to whatever degree it is unforced, "I forgive you. I forgive you." It is so painful to put someone out of your heart. Have mercy on you, forgive them. As this ability to invite them into your heart to be touched by the possibility of forgiveness increases with repetition, there seems more space for them and, quite noticeably, more space for yourself as well. Forgiveness is an act of self-compassion. Let their image float in your consciousness surrounded by intentions for their well-being. And when the work of the moment feels complete, bid them farewell for a while.

Expanding the practice not just to offer but to receive forgiveness, we next bring to mind someone who has resentment toward us. Someone we may have caused pain to in the past is invited into the trembling heart so as to encourage the possibility of their forgiveness. Notice any part of the mind that holds back from asking forgiveness, that perhaps feels it deserves to suffer. Have mercy. Watch closely the tightening in the grief-stricken, guilt-ridden, gut. Soften, let the old ghosts float in something gentler and less harmful than the clenched fist of self-judgment. Soften the belly, and for just a moment remember what pain you yourself were in when you caused difficulty for another. Remember the fear, distrust, confusion, and even defensive indifference that supported your unskillful act. Feel the pain it may have caused. And meet that pain with compassion and forgiveness. And let the mind, raw with its pain, begin to sink into the ocean of compassion that is the ever-forgiving heart as it vows not to repeat those acts that have caused harm to others. It is here that the practice of making amends is cultivated.

Speaking to the person we may have harmed, listening to their side of the story, feeling a great desire for their well-being, say to them, "I ask your forgiveness." As awkward and painful as it may be, ask again slowly, "I ask that you forgive me for whatever I may have done, intentionally or unintentionally, that caused you pain."

Let yourself be touched by the possibility of their forgiveness. Don't resist it, don't cling to your self-righteous suffering, let it go. Let go of this state of mind that has caused so many of the problems that you now see, as life shortens, are in need of some resolution. Let the forgiveness in. Nothing is too good to be true, let yourself be forgiven. To the degree you insist that you must suffer, you insist on the suffering of others as well. And if you imagine that your suffering and the suffering of others are somehow separate, you are not seeing, on even the most basic level, how your suffering causes suffering, and how you suffer the pains of others. "I ask your forgiveness for whatever difficulty I may have caused you through my fear, arrogance, distrust, greed, or ignorance."

Allow yourself to feel the waves of forgiveness transmitted from their heart to yours. Let them in, let yourself be forgiven, and when the moment has passed bid them a grateful farewell. Say good-bye for now and send them on their way with many blessings.

As this process of sending and receiving forgiveness matures, we eventually come to the point where we can turn and say "I forgive you" to ourselves. It is a radical departure from the hells to which we have become so accustomed.

Calling yourself by your own first name, say "I forgive you" to yourself. Have mercy on yourself. Let yourself back into your heart. Watch how the mind, so insistent on its own suffering, clings to its pain, refuses to let go, perhaps even trying to dissuade you from freedom by saying that self-forgiveness is self-indulgent. It knows just how to get you. It has become sharpened from years of self-cruelty. Forgive that too. Send forgiveness into even the unforgiving mind. Soften around that hardness. Do it no injury or insult, just let it float in a kindness it feared would never arise. Like every pain it simply wants our attention. Let your loving kindness flow into it, into yourself, for the benefit of all whose life path you share and for the ground beneath your feet. And send that mercy, that loving kindness, that forgiveness, out into the world. Let it radiate out to all who share the triumphs and defeats of life. Feeling the heart expand to embrace all sentient beings, say, "May all beings be free from suffering. May all beings be at peace."

Let the boundaries of your care and love dissolve to include all beings on every level of existence, whispering in the open heart, "May all beings everywhere, seen and unseen, be free from suffering. May they know the absolute joy of their absolute nature."

"May all beings take the opportunity of existence to become free."

"*May all beings overcome suffering and discover the ever-uninjured essence of their true heart.*"

For an exceptional exploration of traditional loving kindness practice, read Lovingkindness: The Revolutionary Art of Happiness by Sharon Salzberg.

GRATITUDE

It was quite noticeable during the one-year experiment that although I was attempting to live as though there were no tomorrow, so to speak, I nonetheless had to commit to lectures and workshops a year or more in the future. Actually, as I write this in spring 1996, three months after my due date, the taste of each new morning is that much sweeter and the air that much fresher.

The one-year living/dying practice increased my gratitude for life considerably, and by enhancing a sense of presence seems to have deepened the senses as well. Roses have never smelled so beautiful, nor are they even required in order to receive their perfume. I have never heard such music as in the song that sings itself in the still small voice within. I have never lived a life so much larger than death.

Gratitude is the state of mind of thankfulness. As it is cultivated, we experience an increase in our "sympathetic joy," our happiness at another's happiness. Just as in the cultivation of compassion, we may feel the pain of others, so we may begin to feel their joy as well. And it doesn't stop there. We begin to feel a growing sense of gratitude for whatever happiness, great or small, that comes to those around us.

Practicing gratitude increases our appreciation for life. It brings balance to those parts of the self that have cultivated attachment to our suffering, causing us to feel victimized by life, making God's imagined dial tone all too appealing. Although we might suspect that gratitude would cause us to tarry, to grasp at more, it actually potentiates our letting go into life and death with an open heart.

Gratitude is the highest form of acceptance. Like patience, it is one of the catalytic agents, one of the alchemist's secrets, for turning dross to gold, hell to heaven, death to life. Where there is gratitude we get the teaching. Where there is resistance we discover only that it keeps us painfully ignorant. Of course, if we had enough acceptance to explore our nonacceptance, if we learned nothing but that resistance amplified our suffering, we would be eternally grateful.

We cannot feign gratitude any more than we can pretend forgiveness. Gratitude is a way of seeing, of being. It is a response from our innate wisdom to our accumulated confusion. It is the luminous ground on which we plant our temporary feet.

As I reviewed my life with soft eyes, meeting moment after moment of the flickering past with a nonjudgmental awareness, I experienced healings in quite unexpected ways. I met myself with more kindness and a willingness not to suffer for the times I had "fallen."

This growth of compassion taught me a considerably more merciful level of what "detachment" really means. This is a much misunderstood term that careens through spiritual practice throughout the world. It is a word that sends the unintentionally suffering mind shuffling off to the madhouse. At least that is what it felt like to me when, at nineteen, I could not comprehend how to become "detached" from such deep feelings and still be alive, much less write a poem.

Our misinterpretation of that honorable teaching can stop us in our tracks. Until we discover that detachment does not mean an indifference to the pain in ourselves and the people around us, but rather a settling back to observe with clarity and perspective that which calls out for healing. Gradually it becomes clear that detachment means letting go and nonattachment means simply letting be.

As the life review began to produce a remarkably parental kindness toward my earlier miscreancies, a certain beneficent detachment began to arise. It was as if my life had occurred to my only child. It was both more and less than "my own" life, something I could approach wholeheartedly without need for a buffer. The gradual healing process of the forgiveness and gratitude practices expands our life. We become noticeably less concerned with praise or blame, fame or shame. We fear even less that if we get too close to certain parts of our life it might "burst our bubble" and we might discover ourselves unworthy of salvation.

In whatever condition and conditioning we find ourselves, whether we have just won the lottery or discovered we have only a year to live, there is a basic, even essential, gratitude contemplation that is always appropriate. It is an expansion of the process of sending gratitude to individuals. It acknowledges the enormous opportunity of being alive and awakening to our true nature.

AN ESSENTIAL GRATITUDE

CONTEMPLATION

FOR GOOD TIMES AND BAD

Find a comfortable place to sit and settle in there.

Notice the levels of comfort as you soften into your body.

Feel this human body you sit in, this body in which consciousness experiences an ongoing sense of presence.

Explore this precious human body that momentarily houses your enormity.

Feel the moment-to-moment unfolding of sensation in the flow of consciousness.

Feel the moment-to-moment unfolding of consciousness in the steady light of awareness.

This body is the laboratory for the spirit. Send blessings into it.

Thank it for the opportunities it offers.

View the body with gratitude and the appreciation we might have for a simple old vase in which we daily find new flower arrangements.

My first teacher often remarked about the extraordinary good fortune of having a human body in which to continue our deepest work. He was speaking of the grace of being able to understand the nature of grace. He was referring to the struggle and joy of discovering the universal in the separate. The profound healing when the seemingly separate dissolves into the evidently whole.

Grateful for this moment in which to see how we see, to feel how we feel (having, for instance, body patterns more readily explorable than some of the states of mind they accompany), to know that we do not know and that in all our knowing there is nothing that could not be known on a deeper level.

How very fortunate we are to have this moment in this body with some intuitive acknowledgment of that which goes beyond our understanding.

Even with the difficulties, even with the confusion, how blessed we are to be here. And how profound these teachings we took birth for.

Grateful for the kindness of loved ones. Grateful for the moments of joy. Grateful for the clarity that arises even during pain. Grateful for the blessings, great and small. Grateful that our pain is no greater than it is.

Thankful for our Great Heart and the capacity to become whole. Thankful for the angels met along the way. Thankful to be living in a world and a time, in which the value of compassion cannot be overlooked. Thankful to be born into this world of "shit and sunshine."

Grateful that among the billions now on this planet our hearts are so drawn by the possibility of liberation. Grateful for the path that has brought us each so far. Grateful for the love and the grace that spontaneously emerge from our true heart.

Grateful for our inheritance, that even though "happiness" is something of a superstition, joy is our birthright.

Grateful for the sense of presence. Gratitude for simply being.

Grateful for our lotus rising even imperceptibly through dark waters on its way toward the light.

Gratitude for the healings that accompany our birth and death. Gratitude for the Great Light that dawns with the Point of Remembrance. Gratitude for the beneficent process.

19

KEEPING A

JOURNAL

As a means of increasing awareness of, and thus healing, the subtler states noticed in the life review, it is recommended you keep a journal. I began writing what became this book about six weeks after beginning the one-year experiment, coincidentally around Valentine's Day. Such journaling may take the form of poems or paintings, prose or letters to friends, anything that records our feelings and can be referred to at another time.

Recording states of mind in a journal is a written form of noting. For most of our lives we have given so little attention to our mental states that we hardly know anything about our inner process. Investigating in writing the origination and interdependence of states of mind can be quite illuminating. When we observe a state of mind and appreciate that anger or fear are not single states but processes that include such other states as pride, doubt, helplessness, and self-protection, it is possible to start relating *to* these states instead of just *from* them.

To reinforce the clarity and potentials of a healing life review it is suggested we keep a journal of the dozens of constantly recurring states of mind that are the superstructure of life. Note fear when it arises, exploring its process. Note anger as the belly tightens. Note moments of liking or disliking, of acceptance or annoyance. Note the predominant replays the mind has become most accustomed to, such as avarice (wanting more), lust (wanting that!), conceit (vanity and righteousness), envy (coveting it), jealousy (coveting them), worry, helplessness, hopelessness, and general dismay.

But this is only one side of the record. We also note appreciation, clarity, insight, joy, compassion, equanimity, rapture, tranquillity, and love. "Journaling your states for all you're worth," as one woman put it.

Keeping a journal of our most distinct memories as well as the states of mind they engender, their emotions, and their attitudes, can become a very skillful tool for liberating old holdings into a new realm of self-discovery. When I began to realize that the only way to become more loving was to explore that which caused me to be unloving, I did not relish the task. Noting which states of mind obstruct my openness, I began focusing on even the slightest arising of these states so they might be met at their inception well before they could eclipse the heart.

What at this moment is your state of mind? And why are you not altogether certain? Remember there is nothing we know that we couldn't know at a deeper level. Go to that level. Draw a map in your journal.

20

ALTARING

YOUR LIFE

In the years we offered ten-day residential Conscious Living/Conscious Dying intensives, we used to have a long table at one end of the room on which we displayed photographs of some of the patients' dying processes we had shared with the group. On breaks and in between sessions, many of the participants gathered around the series of pictures of Chris and Donna and Mark and Leslie and remarked on the beauty of Leslie's eyes or the Christ-like glow on dead Chris's countenance, or the poignant photo of Donna's children beside her sickbed.

One day we noticed a note left for Mark and another later in the day to Donna. The next day photos of some of the participants dead loved ones began to appear, in addition to flowers, poems, wedding rings, amulets, and drawings of beloved teachers, parents, and children. The following day a piano bench had been placed atop the table and covered with a prayer cloth and a baby's blanket to form a second tier of what became over the next week an amazing altar to life and death, to grieving and gratitude, to forgiveness and appreciation.

Over the next few days it grew a third tier draped with the mementos of moments shared with those whose presence had passed: photos of infants in their cribs and in their coffins, teething rings and teddy bears, wedding pictures, a photo of a boisterous quartet of youthful comrades heading off to Vietnam, and a drawing of the dress uniforms hanging years later in that closet to which none returned. A telegram that another son would not come home. A yellowed charcoal drawing of Auschwitz. Letters from dying lovers. A farewell from a father to his daughter. Birth, wedding, graduation, and death announcements. Faded photos of long-ago family reunions. The mug last sipped from by a dying twin. Hair clippings. A beloved grandmother's recipe for spaetzle.

For years thereafter, when preparing the hall for a workshop, tables were placed in a corner and draped with colorful cloths and a few vases of flowers. Before the beginning meditation had begun, baby teeth and worn slippers and photos of couples (only one of which was alive to attend the workshop) began to blossom on the altar. By lunchtime the altar had become the gathering point for many. They had built a temple to grieving, and were using it very skillfully. At one workshop the altar grew to a five-tiered masterwork shimmering with votive candles that honored in every way imaginable the joy and grief of the consequences of love. It was a Potala to our broken heart and the spirit that heals it.

Many built small altars (or what in Asia are called "pujas") in their bedrooms or meditation corners. Some put them in the kitchen or living room so the whole family could participate in their organic evolution. It was not so much an honoring of what had passed as a celebration of the living present.

Some family altars display report cards and traffic tickets, birthday cards, and cogent news clippings. On others, newspaper photos of the Oklahoma federal building in flames became the first remembrance of compassion each morning. For still others it was the videotape box of *The Little Princess* that their daughter had watched repeatedly while she was dying.

Personal altars can become a substantial accompaniment to a life review. Photos and mementos provide a mirror for our life and times. An altar that honors the work still to be done as well as that already completed.

In the cultivation of my one-year-of-life-left *puja*, besides photos of loved ones and objects of remembrance, I included a book by a person from whom I differed considerably, just to keep me humble, as well as the photograph of someone I wished I had treated with more kindness. My apologetic monologue toward that person became less guilt-induced and more cordial until one day in contemplation of the altar, quite unexpectedly, we seemed to share a moment of remembrance and forgiveness that lifted a great heaviness from my heart.

Build an altar to your life. Let it be an artful counterpart to the journal in which you record your changing states of mind. Like the journal, the altar constantly evolves with each memory and insight. It grows and changes over the years just as we do; in fact, precisely as we do. It is the endless sky in which impermanence floats.

21

LIVING IN

THE BODY

Before we can leave the body effortlessly we have to inhabit it fully. A remarkable means of heightening life as
well as preparing for death is to enter the body wholeheartedly, sensation by sensation. It is a gentle guiding of
awareness through the body beginning at the top of the head
and extending to the tip of the toes. In colloquial Buddhism
this is called a "sweeping" meditation, partially because the
awareness sweeps through the body and partly because it
sweeps from under the rug much that has been sequestered
there. Awareness resuscitates those parts of the body that have
become numbed by fear and encourages their participation in
the whole. It also balances the tension in areas bursting with
imprisoned energy. It brings the disparate aspects of the body,
loved and unloved, into harmony.

Exploring the field of sensation we call the body allows us
to see that we are more than this body, that we are the awareness which inhabits and explores it. Close attention to sensation is a means of being present for, and through, the letting go
of the body. It is an encouragement of life to enter the body

moment by moment, sensation by sensation that ultimately
can enable it to find its way back out just as consciously.

A MEDITATION ON LIFE IN THE BODY

*Quieting enough to feel that subtle sensation just between the scalp
and the skullcap, let awareness settle at the top of the head. Feel the hardness of the bone and the softness of the scalp. Note their different qualities.
Braille your way into the center of the sensations that arise there. Feel the
warp and woof of their texture.*

*Slowly sweep from sensation to sensation in the brow, around the
eyes, in the cheeks, behind the ears, within the lips and tongue and mouth.
Moving perhaps tooth by tooth to discern any subtle changes from one to
another. Just observing. Just allowing awareness to progress through the
body like a lamplighter through a familiar village at dusk, illuminating
the way for our evening stroll.*

*Allow your awareness to move slowly through the throat, noting its
dank warmth and long-denied dry spots. Acknowledge that it is fear even
more than the well-rippled esophagus that keeps it ridged. Observe each
sensation as the muscles of the neck spread out to form the shoulders. Feel
the weight of the arms hanging there. Gradually sweep down each arm
through the biceps, elbow, forearm, wrist, and into each individual finger.
Feel life scintillating in the fingertips.*

*And down through the torso, feeling within each organ, heart, lungs,
stomach, liver, kidneys, bladder—the sensations arising there.*

*And down the spine, feeling the subtle variations from vertebra to ver-
tebra.*

*Nothing to create—just a receptive awareness that focuses on what-
ever presents itself for subtler exploration.*

And down into the lower abdomen, investigating areas of tension as well as openness with an equal-hearted satisfaction at being inside the process from which we have felt subtly excluded for so long. Inside the life inside our body. And gradually through the hips and genitalia, noting any tension or exclusion of the anal sphincter. (In this process we can exclude nothing if we are to become whole.)

And down into each leg individually, through the thigh and knee and calf and ankle into the remarkable splay of metacarpals that work the foot and allow us to shift back and forth in bewilderment at this process of reentering the body. And into each toe and the sole of each foot.

Then, to take this technique to another level, practice dying out of that body on the way back up from the toes to the top of the head. It is the top of the head, by the way, that is considered the most skillful point of departure at the time of death.

Watch sensation after sensation dissolve into an awareness that sweeps upward into an increasing sense of spaciousness.

Let each sensation disappear as though that part of the body was dissolving as well.

Rise toward the crown of the head, gathering awareness as you go.

Let the life force follow the open conduit just established, finding its way home, sensation by sensation up the spine, through the heart and throat, and into the top of the head.

The intention of this body-sweeping practice is twofold. First, to allow one to reinhabit the body fully. Second, to offer one the opportunity, when the time is ripe, to leave the body completely behind. It intensifies a certain aliveness while providing a channel for the life force to exit cleanly when the body has become something of a mess. It's just another play with life that eases our death.

WITH DEATH
JUST OVER
MY
SHOULDER

For almost a year I have, as they say, kept death over my left shoulder. It has made me more alive. It has brought a deep appreciation and joy to impermanence, the joy of playing close attention. It invites me to participate in the ever-changing present. It says time is a fallacy.

I have had no slight teaching about impermanence from the ongoing teachings of the death of my first teacher, Rudi, almost thirty years ago, in an airplane accident; my second teacher, Sujata, years later of AIDS; and another teacher incapacitated by a stroke. Also my mentors, Ramana Maharshi, Neem Karoli Baba, and Mahasi Sayadaw—all long dead. But then again, it's often easier to get in touch with them now than it was before: no call waiting, no long-distance static.

As Ondrea said the other day when I mentioned how many life companions had died or were dying, "And that's only the beginning. From now on until it's your turn, you are going to continue to receive calls that all your friends are dying."

You would think that with all the deaths I've attended and the counseling of the dying I've offered over the last twenty years, I would be fully prepared. Yet it was illuminating during the one-year life/death experiment to notice how much more aware I was becoming of my own mortality. Clearly no one else's death, however terrible or profound, can fully remove our own denial, or the confusion that wishes never to die and has forgotten that it never shall.

As one woman, dying in isolation and too much pain, said, "Let's see how Stephen would do under these circumstances!" She was right on the mark. Let's see indeed! Let's see now, before it's too late, how I may be magic-thinking my way toward death, what I have secretly swept under the rug, how I delude myself that I "know death." Now is the time to observe how we may count on dying on a "good day," how we delay the work that remains to be done.

A few years ago, a woman attending our "Conscious Living/Conscious Dying" weekend workshop was killed in an automobile accident on her way home. Many people lamented her "bad luck," but something in Ondrea and me rejoiced at her good fortune at having been serendipitously prepared for what might otherwise have caught her unawares. I still can't tell whether her death was tragedy or grace.

LETTING GO

OF CONTROL

M any people do not feed themselves their last meal, or flush their last bowels. Often the body's strength dwindles as it slowly approaches death. If we are fortunate we are aided by caregivers.

When our body is not responding the way we wish it would and we feel we aren't the person we once were, it is often difficult to be served in such a manner. Being looked after reinforces our sense of helplessness and a lifetime's resistance to such feelings. There is something in us that finds it easier to serve than be served. It is that occasional sense of powerlessness we have attempted to avoid and has thus grown unabated. We need to open to our helplessness and explore it.

We may feel hopeless but we are never really helpless; we can always soften and surrender into what is and participate in it as best we can. We certainly may not be able to control the situation, but we may be able to relinquish some of the resistance to it that turns the difficult to the intolerable.

How will we keep our heart open when we can no longer

move our hands? Practice helplessness. The following are a few exercises that can be practiced repeatedly to that end:

The first is simply to help define our reliance on control and the unexplored pathways of habit: Let whoever usually leads during close dancing follow instead. It is a hundred laughs and a multitude of potential tears. We find it very difficult if we don't soften our belly and surrender into the dance.

The second exercise is a bit more to the point: Leave your hands by your sides and let yourself be fed. Also let yourself be dressed by another. Watch frustration. Do not lift your hands.

The third practice is blind walking. Allow someone you trust to lead you blindfolded around the house. Watch distrust and fear. To take the surrender to another level practice this one by yourself, walk alone, blindfolded, in a dark house.

The fourth is to spend a day or some substantial part thereof doing nothing, absolutely nothing: not speaking, not watching television, not listening to music, eating little or nothing; no sex, no drugs, no rock and roll. Watch the unstimulated mind display restlessness. Soften your belly and surrender into the dance.

JULY

J ust over halfway through the year I received an invitation to my fortieth high school reunion. Along with it came a list of old classmates, their addresses, and their present status. About one in nine had died.

And news in New York of the dying of colleagues and spiritual friends. Luke gone on ahead to delight Paradise with the dharma. Mark, deeply cancered, clear as a temple bell, exploring the technology of consciousness transference upon death known as *phowa* in his long practice of Tibetan Buddhism. And Tom, who doesn't know if he'll live out the month, driving away on his final pilgrimage.

It is said if we could see the whole truth we would, on any given day, be able to witness hundreds of thousands of spirits departing the earth like so many lightning bolts reaching outward. From deep space this is said to look like a fireworks display on a well-celebrated Independence Day. Just in case I was forgetting the 250,000 other people who will die the same day I do, July was full of the deaths of old friends and patients. Deciduous leaves piled at the foot of the great tree.

While reflecting on the absence of friends of my youth, the mind realized with a start that it was more than halfway through the "last year of life," that more time had elapsed than remained. And it began to bargain for an extension. It threatened to sue. It insisted that the "last year" had not begun until six weeks after New Year's, when the process got up to full steam and the writing had begun. It argued that it had until next Valentine's Day to live and did not have to let go before then. I gave the mind a cookie and a warm glass of milk and told it to soften its belly and prepare to die. It grumbled for a moment, then burst into laughter. It was learning to trust the process.

TOM

I had not seen Tom since Haight-Ashbury.
The note said he had a mouth full of cancer.

He answered the phone and we instantly connected.
He said the wife and kids were "hanging in there"
but so was the cancer. He had the best of the worst.
He said he had done everything he could to heal
but a cure did not follow. He sounded a bit lost but,
as he put it, "holding my own."

When I suggested we meditate together he said
he really didn't want his world expanded right now,
that he had his hands full with it the size it was.

Bought a '67 V.W. van for the final pilgrimage
back to his childhood home on the East Coast
and was in the midst of giving everything away,
said there wasn't much because he had always
                been an optimist.

Heading north to his parents' graves near Seattle,
then due east for the slow drive through the long woods home.

Almost thirty years ago standing knee-deep in the south fork
of the Eel River I acted minister for their wedding.
A chronicler of his times,
            photographer of the Haight,
            Woodstock and the Chicago riots,
whose times were running out.

Now they were packing for the journey.
"When they tell you you've only got a few months to live
it seems like there's an awful lot to do.
But as soon as I get my carburetor tuned
I'm off on a road trip to parts unknown."

26

WHO DIES?

We go through life pretending to be real. We are told from every guarded corner that we are supposed to be "a solid citizen," someone of merit. We are relieved that no one seems to notice that we hardly exist, that we are only a thought here and there, some feelings floating through, a few frames of color-faded memory, a tingling in the fingertips, a bewilderment of opposing desires and beliefs. We go on bravely posturing, incredulous that no one sees through our ruse. Impersonating what we imagine a "solid" human being to be, we just keep guessing and taking pointers from the other actors. Everyone seems so much more real to us than we do to ourselves, we wonder in the midst of our conflicted conditioning how this unruly tangle is going to face death, much less an afterlife.

We fear we are not real enough to die and so begin to investigate what life might truly be. We turn inward and like an absolute beginner, taking nothing for granted and accepting nothing secondhand, we enter the flow of consciousness to see who is doing all this thinking and what is observing it all.

Like the ideal scientist with perfect "don't-know mind," entertaining no preconceptions, open to any possibility, completely vulnerable to the truth, we examine everything. One of the first beliefs we come across is that the only reason we imagine we will die is because we are convinced we were born. But we cannot trust hearsay! We must find out for ourselves. Were we born? Or was that just the vessel in which our timelessness momentarily resides. What indeed was born? And who dies?

When we look into the contents of consciousness by which we define ourselves, we find that nothing lasts very long. There is no thought we have ever had that did not have a beginning, a middle, and an end. Everything in consciousness is constantly dying and being reborn. One thought dissolves into another. One feeling evolves into the next. There seems nothing permanent, nothing that is not already dying. And we wonder in the midst of such impermanence if there is anything "real" enough to survive death.

Life lasts only a moment. Then another moment arises and dissolves into the flow. We live our life from instant to instant never knowing what the next unfolding will provide. But then something in all this catches our eye. We realize that every experience of our lifetime has been impermanent, except one. That there is an unchanging spaciousness in which all our changes float. How could we have overlooked the obvious so completely? From the moment that we became aware we were aware, whether at the breast or in the womb or the day before yesterday, there has been a single constant no matter what else was happening. There has been a consistent sense of simply being. Not being "this" or "that" but the "thusness" into which our treasured this and thats cannot be prevented from disappearing. In fact, this underlying sense of being is as present as we are, and does not change from birth to death. It is the constant hum of being in our ever-changing cells. When we look directly at this sense of suchness, when we enter it, when we sit quietly within it, we discover that it is endless. If we ask ourselves whether this sense of being seems to have a beginning and an end, whether it was born and is capable of dying, we can say only that we may have been previously misinformed about the deathless nature of our essence, that the news of our death had been highly exaggerated, as Huck might put it.

Don't try to name it; you'll only start a holy war. That's why some call it the Unnameable. It is pure awareness before consciousness begins to stir. It is the space between thoughts. It is the ocean in which our tiny bubble floats. It is the formlessness upon which form depends, the deathless which dies again and again just to prove it never dies.

We have been taught that we need our body to exist, but it is just the other way around. When who we really are departs from who we thought we were, the body collapses and instantly becomes a disposal problem. It is the ultimate in natural conservation in which the container is discarded but the contents are recycled.

Anything that can die, will. That which cannot, won't. Find out for yourself how to take the teaching from each of these aspects of being and how to integrate the whole into a heart that cares and serves. That which is impermanent attracts compassion. That which is not provides wisdom.

What makes you think you were born and what makes you think you will die? Watch such thoughts closely and notice the enormity in which they unfold.

We have gone mad looking for a solid center but there is none. Our center is vast space. Nothing to die and nothing to hang your hat on.

27

ORIGINAL

FACE

Some people believe that your heart stops when you die. Others sense that it continues. Which makes the question not just what, or who, dies but what doesn't? What becomes of that which animated the body? Where did it come from and where does it go?

In Zen training the teacher will sometimes ask, "What was your face before you were born?" What is your original nature? What is it in you that was never born and does not die? The question often takes students by surprise. They try to peer out of the back of their eyeballs to see some visage within. They see only acquired confusion.

Our original face is our faceless presence. When reflected in the mirrorworks of the mind it is that which experiences thought and feeling. It is the light by which consciousness is lit. It peers through the mask of personality and offers life.

To discover one's original face is to see behind the mask. Beyond thought and thinking, beyond the known, beyond impermanence, is the ever-present unnameable thusness of being: our timeless, deathless, energetic essence. To get even a glimpse of our original face can be as startling as it is liberating. It extends our life to eons. It transforms death.

You have stared into a mirror a thousand times to look at the face from which you stare. You have surveyed and appraised this face acquired with birth from all the perspectives of the personality that came along with the bargain. And still you cannot see most of yourself: the countenance of your original nature.

Many speak of "out-of-body" experiences, in which they hovered above their corporal realm and watched the goings-on with ease and bemusement. These things sometimes happen to those with serious illness, and particularly those on their deathbed. They are reassured that they do not have to depend upon their disintegrating bodies for existence. They notice that there seems to be a lighter body, even a body of light, within the physical body that is independent of the heavy outer shell.

Of perhaps even greater importance is what occurs when one has an "other-than-the-body" experience. An endless opening into the vastness of being that does not mistake itself for any body at all, astral or otherwise. A healing that stops nowhere.

This is a direct experience of the dynamic stillness of our formless essence that is not dependent on any body, subtle or gross. As they say in Buddhism, "Emptiness is not nothing, it's just no thing."

To explore this subject more deeply read Zen Mind, Beginner's Mind *from the vast heart of Suzuki Roshi.*

ORIGINAL FACE
CONTEMPLATION

Sitting quietly, feel what sits there.

Explore this body you sit in.

Observe the scintillating field of sensation we call the body.

Notice sensation's wordless quality.

Its sense of simply being humming throughout the body.

Go within sensation to that subtle presence by which the sensation is known. Feel the sensation within sensation.

Settle into that sense of being, of aliveness vibrating in each cell.

Rest in being.

In the silence of sensation a sense of presence is discovered.

Notice how any thought arising clutters that simple suchness and makes it think it is that solid something, that solid someone, to which suffering adheres. And loses its spacious context.

Rest in being.

Just sit quietly and know. Let awareness sink into itself. Know what knows.

Experience directly that sense by which you imagine you exist.

Enter it wholeheartedly. Sit in the center of that hum.

Does it have a beginning? Does it have an ending?

Or is there just a sense of endless being, unborn and undying?

Don't ask the mind, which always limits itself with definitions; ask the heart, which cannot name it but always is it.

Rest in being.

Feel within that timeless presence the vastness of being, the unnameable essence from which consciousness is produced. It is the common experience of our universal mystery.

Since birth there has been only one experience that has never changed: the experience of simply being. Not being this or that. Just being.

Since the moment we became aware we were aware there has been a single ongoing experience underlying all else. It is our original face. The fire from which our tiny spark was thrown.

Rest in the essential illumination of being.

Letting go of all that is impermanent, including the idea of impermanence, enter directly the whoosh of being.

Acknowledging that even our immortality cannot defy our mortality, let go of that which dies, and discover what remains.

When an eighty-year-old Thai meditation master was visiting a center in New England he asked the assembled students, "What is still there after an enlightened person dies?" When a monk offered the orthodox reply that nothing remained, the teacher stopped him and said, "No, the truth remains!"

What is that truth we essentially are which does not die? What is our original nature?

And how does sinking into the presence by which we remain present answer that inquiry?

Recognize that awareness is your original nature before consciousness is born. That consciousness depends on the presence of awareness, but awareness depends on nothing, it simply is.

Rest in being.

See that which sees looking through the eyes of our original face.

Watch with your true eyes the appearance of an essential wisdom and a compassion so great that no one you love will ever die alone again.

And neither will you.

AFTER-DEATH
EXPERIENCES

Many speak of "after-death" experiences, but this is a misnomer. What they are referring to are "after-dying" experiences, or perhaps "during-death" experiences. An after-death experience would be rebirth.

There has been much discussion of late about these experiences. Raymond Moody, Kenneth Ring, and numerous others have explored the stories of those resuscitated from "clinical death." They have interviewed hundreds of people who spoke of floating free of their bodies, hearing themselves pronounced dead, and headed across some barrier or through some tunnel, past long-departed loved ones, drawn magnetically toward a brilliant light that emanated an all-consuming peace and an all-embracing love. Most personified the great light as Jesus or Buddha, or God herself. Some children have spoken of meeting Santa Claus. A few teenagers described meeting an admired cartoon Superhero. And for the astonished atheist, who mistakenly believed that the existence of an afterlife was dependent on the existence of a God, when in truth it depends only on existence itself, perhaps a smiling gray-haired Einstein waiting with a cup of tea to sit and talk it all out. Most that returned from such an experience came back with three very precious insights: an increased appreciation of life, a diminished fear of death, and a new sense of purpose. Now that's a life review for you!

As wonderful and reassuring as all that is, there is, however, a tragic note. How few returning were so well prepared, so familiar with their own great nature that they recognized their original face blazing there before them? How few knew to strip naked the clingings to "name and form" and enter directly this unique opportunity? How many who suffered from a case of mistaken identity before death were able to break through it afterward?

Most people are wholly unprepared for their enormity. In death as in life most retreat along habitual pathways, no matter how painful, just to find a recognizable neighborhood no matter how unsatisfying. We think too small. In fact, thought itself is not big enough to encompass the truth. Like our original face, or the indefinable miracle of being, we can never fully "know" it, but we can always fully be it. In the Old Testament it says that we can know God but we can never be God. In my experience it is just the other way around. We can experience that level of consciousness, that vastness of being, whose rapture, for lack of a better term, we might call God, but we cannot describe afterward what that experience was. We tend to describe what it wasn't. And it wasn't something that could be captured in thought. It was neither form nor the absence of form. It was not in time but of the timelessness from which time is extracted. "It was like nothing I had ever experienced before but it was totally familiar."

The whole truth cannot be held in thought but its aftertaste can last a lifetime. Thought is to the mind what your momentary face is to your original countenance. Thought simply describes itself. For the truth we need something bigger and more intuitive that, even when the mind is confused, knows its way home by heart.

To discover our original face is the work that needs to be done now before our latest face slips from our skull and lies staring helplessly up at us from our deathbed.

As mentioned earlier, various sacred books describe methods by which we can elude the personifications of our continued fear of death even after we die. Our fear of being harmed seems to be reinforced by any identification whatsoever with any body whatsoever, no matter how subtle or luminous. Your original face has no body. It doesn't even have a face.

Many shudder when they speak about the possibilities of a cruel afterworld. We suspect our life is not up to the scrutiny. We fear punishment. We imagine death as altogether different from life, although it is constructed from the same projections of mind.

We have read a number of religious scenarios about what might happen after death and are saddened by the degree to which punishment is considered necessary and even holy. There is nothing noble about suffering except the love and forgiveness with which we meet it. Many believe that if they are suffering they are closer to God, but I have met very few who could keep their heart open to their suffering enough for that to be true. Most who talk about hell are in it at the time. In my experiences with the dying and into death, much less the visions beyond, I have seen nothing of the sort. In fact, concepts of dying into a heaven or hell seem a good deal more political than spiritual. The closest thing I found to hell was the fearful attachment to heaven on the deathbed: the lack of trust in the process. Hell is the obscured heart.

But even hell can lead to paradise when it is recognized with mercy and allowed to float unjudged in consciousness. Such is the story of the dying Tibetan lama surrounded by appreciative students who notices that they are praying for him to be reborn in heaven realms. Raising a feeble hand he said, "Don't pray that I be reborn in heaven. Pray that I be reborn in hell, for where is compassion and wisdom more needed?"

If the concept of hell stimulates your compassion, if one recognizes the hell that so many are in, it can be a powerful practice to direct loving kindness into that darkness. It can elicit service to your sisters and brothers. It can encourage the heart to stay open and available under even the most difficult circumstances.

Fears of hellish karmas distress many but karma is not punishment. It is simply evolutionary momentum propelled from teaching to teaching. It is a beneficent process often more recognizable in perception than in events. Our karma does not so much create what happens to us as how we deal with it. Karma is our increasing capacity for problem-solving on increasingly deepening levels. There is no retribution in karma, just a persistent reminding, until we get the teaching, to let go of our suffering. It is a road map to liberation that warns us where potholes have previously appeared in the road and skillfully points out how to elude potential detours through hell. Karma is for the emerging spirit what an accurate diagnosis is for an unknown illness: an opportunity to recognize what blocks healing and a chance to become whole once again.

I recall some years ago being invited to speak about death and dying to a group of Westerners who were practicing Tibetan Buddhism. As they spoke about the possibilities of the after-realms, you could feel the collective belly tighten. Fear and disquietude filled the room. They felt much trepidation about "crossing the threshold" because of their partial understanding of *The Tibetan Book of the Dead* and other such texts. The room was thick with ignorance and confusion. I wanted to laugh but instead suggested that if they believed in reincarnation, they had to recognize that they have been through this process many times before, and had come out quite well this time around, considering their interest in clarity and compassion. I pointed out how much more wisdom they had uncovered to add to their forward momentum, and that the more we practice how to have a bad day well, the better a day it will be.

When we stop protecting ourselves from life, each moment takes on a new significance. We come to treasure our being even more than our becoming. Each moment of remembering is precious, the eternal moment in which there is no other.

Even our insights, held to for protection, can imprison us. In fact, even enlightenment does not perfect the personality, only the point of view. It cleans the dust from our eyes but it doesn't change their color. Buddha said after his final liberation that he had broken the roof beam that held up the roof of his "house," his conditioning, his karma, the self-image. He had deconstructed the cause of suffering that imprisons the mind and obscures the truth, and rested there forever more.

BEYOND THE

HOUSE OF

DEATH

Beyond the wheel of birth and death, beyond concepts that limit our birth and narrow our death lies the truth. That truth is the vastness of being before it condenses into form, the deathless before it appears in the guise of the deathful. It is that into which so many Hindus and Buddhists wish to merge, to end the rounds of life and death, and enter, without interruption, the truth that is beyond name and form.

To keep this deeper truth "as frontlets between thine eyes" is to go beyond even death, much less the mental dioramas of reward and punishment we project as above or below us that are just elaborate forms of our detoxification from life. After a long life of delusion and a severe case of mistaken identity, what some presume to be hell is no more than the difficulty of letting go of our suffering, a sweeping-clear of confusions and doubts. It's a weeding of the garden, a transitional state, temporary and theatrical, before the "point of remembrance" is integrated, which opens the gates of heaven to the degree we can surrender that in us which creates hell. Hell is just a hangover that passes with proper nutrition. It's just detox. It is the anteroom to heaven in the same way heaven is the anteroom to a yet more spacious paradise.

While not stopping at death we need not stop at heaven either. To settle for heaven is to cultivate the attachments of hell. Beyond such polarities lies that which has no opposite, the oneness out of which the One arises. Beyond even the sacred there is the source of the sacred. Beyond our imaginings there is a freedom so enormous and comforting that it makes even paradise seem constricting.

Let no misguided priestcraft stay our pilgrimage. Let us find out for ourselves what lies beyond the walls of our ideas of life and death, beyond the mental constructs that form the superstructure for the house that Buddha speaks of tearing down in order to be free. As for Jesus, there was only one house, his Father's, but even he had to slip outside every once in a while to take a breather.

RETURN

APPEARANCES

I have long wondered about the phenomena of the dead appearing to the living, as in that not uncommon experience in which a recently departed loved one appears in what might be called a "real dream"—"It was so real, it was more than a dream." The visitor says in the same manner exactly the same thing in whatever language spoken, "I'm okay. Everything is okay." What indeed is happening? I have heard these stories dozens of times from children as well as from a wide variety of adults with a wide variety of belief systems. Even those who were certain there was no afterlife, much less those yet more certain that nothing about death could be okay, had the same unexpectedly comforting dream.

So widespread is this experience and so exact the wording that it has long resided in my Don't Know/Real Illusion file. I wondered, if by all accounts the departed moves on to other, subtler realms of being, how he or she might still be experienced in this dense here and now. Considering that these people left their tickets behind, how are they able to reenter the theater?

It was a question that reminded me to stay open to any possibility. And in that willingness to understand there arose one day an interesting thesis, an answer not necessarily the answer. If on another plane someone were in that dream level experiencing him- or herself meeting us again and speaking to us, might not their extraordinary concentration and strong attachment project them through into this one? Perhaps their experience of us in another world becomes our experience of them in this world? Do we meet in the dream that each dreams of the other, living with the consequences of love?

What of plants that burst into flower in the middle of winter a day after a loved one dies? Or impossible messages left on a telephone-answering machine? Or even visitations in which complex predictions are made that turn out to be precisely accurate . . . ? Big don't know! But I do know that when the early stages of grief in which we feel the absolute absence of the departed subsides, and the mind begins to sink into the heart, there arises a sense of absolute inseparability from that person that may well be the two-way bridge across which our dreams are exchanged. If after I died I dreamed with all my heart that I brought you a huge bouquet of flowers, what might happen? And how did you like the card?

31

REINCARNATION

Although most religions can be defined by their concept of the afterworld and how, or whether, reincarnation takes place, none sounds so much more accurate than the others that I would pack accordingly. When the time comes it won't be our religion that guides us, it will be our spirituality. When Buddha was asked what might occur after death, he enumerated dozens of the most popular possibilities, and added that you'd know soon enough. He suggested we should be prepared for anything because even if one of the many were correct and you made a lucky guess, it would still just be an imagining, a model, a mental construct that was more likely to limit wisdom and freedom than produce it. As one very wise old woman said, "I think death is what you think it is." She was as close to the truth as thinking occasionally gets.

Not being attached to a particular afterlife architecture leaves us free of the blinders of expectation. So that when we die we won't be looking around for some familiar fantasy instead of exploring what is directly before us. As one Zen master puts it, "Just go straight."

Obviously, the clarity necessary to navigate through death is cultivated in the midst of life. By investigating what is directly ahead we live so thoroughly in the present that we come to trust the ground beneath our feet and our capacity to stand erect and make our choices from the heart.

Until we find out who was born this time around, it seems irrelevant to seek earlier identities. I have heard many people speak of who they believe they were in previous incarnations, but they seem to have very little idea of who they are in this one. A single life review is difficult enough. Let's take one life at a time. Perhaps the best way to do that is to live as though there were no afterlife or reincarnation. To live as though this moment was all that was allotted.

What difference does it make if nothing happens after death? What if it was, as many people think, just a dial tone, that God hung up on us? Would that in any way diminish the value of mercy and awareness in this moment? Even if this was the only level of existence it would not change the nature of the heart, or the healing to be experienced.

Although I suggest you live as though this was your only moment, in order to decrease attachment to ideas of what is to come, I know from numerous personal and direct experiences that death has a life of its own. My understanding that awareness survives the body is not a belief system, it's just the way it is. It is not the result of some restless philosophy but the product of numerous experiences of, and with, death that coincided from several different directions, including those that accompanied the dying to the threshold and experienced them cross over. Also there were, as remarkable as it sounds, those who somehow visited afterward because they said they wished to offer something in return, and on a rare occasion even shared their death with me. It was from these extraordinary moments that I first experienced the "point of remembrance" and was allowed repeated observation of the dissolution of the elements as they lost sway over a lightening spirit. That which was revealed from these encounters with "the mystery" has been corroborated over the years by depth experiences during extended meditation practice.

Although I know from numerous meditation and "extracurricular" experiences (noted in detail in *Who Dies?*, *Meetings at the Edge*, and *Healing into Life and Death*) that we outlive death, I cannot speak with any assurance about what follows. I have seen from many different angles how the process of dying takes consciousness beyond the body, but that is about as far as I have gone. This could be humorously described as knowing something about death for about an hour or so into the process, or perhaps a day at most.

As I came to experience how the scattered light of awareness converges in the heart to form the Great Light the way the diffused winter sun focuses to a white-hot point through a magnifying glass, I began to recognize this gathering of awareness as the cause of the greatly increased concentration experienced upon death. However, I do not know directly how the converse occurs when the great light breaks into the prismatic effects of other worlds and incarnations, when, like the sun through a crystal, or awareness through consciousness, the one divides into the many.

Yet, when we see how yesterday affects today, how each feeling conditions the next, how the last thought upon falling asleep instigates the first thought upon waking, we get some insight into how rebirth may work. To that end we begin practices like the "last-breath/first-breath" sleep-time exercise. Noting whether we fall asleep on the inbreath or outbreath and whether we awake on the in- or out-breath, though neither are preferable, is a means of sharpening our focus on how the contents of the mind, upon falling asleep, condition the state of the mind upon awakening. It examines the last-thought/first-thought possibilities of reincarnation. It may take a while to see what is occurring one more breath into sleep, but it increases the potential for that kind of lucid dreaming in which you know you are dreaming and thereby have additional latitude of movement. It is good preparation for even our most ordinary day much less one that might set the tone for future days. To awake noting whether we are on the inbreath or outbreath brings us into the immediate present. In the beginning, we may not even remember we wanted to note the waking breath until sometime after lunch. As the practice develops, we remember to remember a little sooner each day, until at last we awake upon awaking to the breath breathing itself in the vastness in which our life unfolds. Last breath informs first breath. Last life creates next.

When we awake mindful of our aliveness and go to sleep contemplating our deathlessness, we are practicing conscious rebirth. In fact, as our last-breath-into-sleep practice develops, we may notice our last thought to be something like "Hey, I'm asleep," and get a fleeting glimpse of what it might be like to be lucid in the dream state. The possibility of awakening within a dream to the fact that we are dreaming, and that the dream is created from our consciousness and susceptible to its whims, is said to be an ideal practice for making conscious decisions in the afterworld. The development of lucid dreaming is considered by many to be one of the most skillful means of preparation for navigating wisely in the afterworld. Last-breath practice can also help. Carlos Castañeda suggested trying to remember in the dream state to look at our hands, having given ourselves that instruction before going to sleep. Finding some trigger for awareness that makes it aware of itself is as much the task of making a dream lucid as of making a lifetime lucid. It is proposed that whether in the sleeping dream or the waking dream any clarity increases the possibility of further clarity. Freud analyzed dreams, Jung investigated dreams, but saints suggest we go yet deeper and use the dream state as an opportunity to rehearse for the show, to get our act together before we go onstage. There is much written on the subject. If it catches your interest, follow that inclination.

It is not as though we live a dozen, a hundred, or even a thousand different lives. We live only one, migrating from body to body, insight to insight, liberation to liberation. Buddha said that our existence cannot be measured in years or even lifetimes, but only in terms of *kalpas* and even *mahakalpas*—the time it takes a dove to wear down an enormous granite mountain by passing over it every hundred years dragging a silk handkerchief in its beak, the time it might take for a Himalayan buzzard to wear away Mount Everest brushing it once a century with its wing feather. A *mahakalpa* is ten thousand times that long. He speaks from direct participation in the whole of our existence, of existence itself, extending through time. He reminds us of the enormous deathlessness of our being-without-end, and that the closer our awareness is to the present moment the closer we are to our timeless essence.

His wisdom reminds us that at the very center of this moment is timelessness and that time just trails off in either direction. He reminds us of the universal in which the personal floats. He encourages us now to become wholly familiar with the light within so as not to be taken by surprise when it shines immense before us. He advises that only acknowledging and entering that light without reserve will prepare us for our enormity.

The Tibetan tradition says that most people are so unaware of their Great Nature that upon seeing the tremendous luminescence of their original face they swoon, trip, and "fall headlong into a womb," taking unconscious rebirth.

The best preparation for reincarnation is to know, from within, that which is deathless, as well as that which remains lifeless.

PETER AND TIM

PETER AND TIM

Peter said,
My prayers don't work anymore!
He and Tim had the virus.
Both were ill for years.

In the hospital, then home a while,
then back again. Sometimes
too sick and frightened to visit.

Lovers taking turns dying.

Up most of the night and most of the day,
attending to each other. Measuring medications,
applying infusions. Dragging fevers
to midnight emergency rooms.
Sometimes bedpans, sometimes too much

pain in the mind / in the body / in the heart
to have made it one more day alone.

It's said that if you truly love someone
you might well wish they died first.
So great is your concern for their smooth passage
that you are willing to go it alone at the end
just so they won't have to.

When I asked Tim,
What will you do if Peter doesn't come home this time?
he said, Die at last.

Peter died at noon on Sunday.

Passing through my heart on his way elsewhere,
he whispered,
              It feels so great to be alive again!
              I was so sick for so long.

TIM AND PETER

Tim's mom called this morning.
Looks like it's the end.
Please keep him in your prayers.

The gardener was dying on the first day of spring.
His beloved partner gone on two months before him
              to prepare the ground,
                    so he would have to bring only the seeds.

In each diminishing breath violets and chrysanthemums.
A great flowering vine growing from his heart
through the top of his head,
like Jack's beanstalk, stretching all the way to Heaven,
emerging into an enormous garden,
    his garden,
        Peter lazy by the fountain.

33

DISPOSING OF

THE CORPSE

At about this point in the one-year experiment it may occur to us that since we have explored "the point of remembrance," and passed through the elements into that which is elementary, entered afterworlds, and practiced reincarnation, perhaps we have missed something. We forgot to get rid of the body.

Ironically, it is this unresolved attachment to the body that continues our fear of death well beyond our dying. As Ramana Maharshi pointed out, if you think you are this body, in the afterworld you will think you are that one. But any body, gross or subtle, that inters consciousness in identification limits our capacity to free awareness to look through the eyes of its original face. This body that depends on our presence for its continued existence is, in a classically codependent manner, attempting to convince us that without it we'd be nothing. It says it is Mount Meru, but in truth it is only a single peak on a mountain range that stretches around the world many times.

When we forgot to dispose of our body we skipped our perfect ending. Of course, this is easy enough to do when there really is none, just a perfect going on. But there we are moldering in the corner, stinking up the room, making it difficult to continue without a foul smell in the psyche.

Clearly, the last step is as important as the first. Just as a newborn's body needs be wiped clean of the remnants of the birthing process, so the new corpse needs to be mindfully and lovingly prepared for its final passage back into the earth's womb. It is more for the living that we straighten out the vacant body house than for the recently departed tenant who has already had his original deposit returned.

So we come to recognize that planning our funeral, as well as communicating our preferred method of disposal, is one of the last collaborations with those we leave behind to tidy up after us.

The exercise of this moment, if not before, is to tidy up before us as much as we can. We create a living will so that loved ones understand our preferred strategy for the endgame, and are saved from agonizing decisions that are our responsibility to make. We check our safety deposit box, actual or imaginary, to make sure that all we intend to leave is in good order. It is a time for codicils from the heart. With our dying will and our living will completed, with letters and tapes of our appreciative farewells left for loved ones, with objects precious to our self-image distributed like a potlatch among the tribe, it is appropriate to be explicit about how we want our dead body to be disposed of. After all, we have only a few more months to experiment.

Would you prefer cremation or burial, to go up in flames or down in moisture? Have you considered the body being laid out on a mountain ledge for what is called a vulture, or sky, burial? Either way, all that is left is just a handful of star dust.

There is considerable discussion about how to supernova that star. Some insist the body must be left undisturbed for days while prayers and guidance are offered, others that it should be interred before the sun sets, others that it should be carried that day to the burning ghats to be libated with the incense and oils that will consume it, yet others that it should be consoled by the world for three days before it is offered up to the divine.

When my teacher Neem Karoli Baba was asked whether burning the body on the day of its death, as is the Indian manner, was skillful he said, "Burn 'em. The sooner they know they are not the body the better." We do not depend on our body for our existence. It is just the other way around. When that which was born departs the vessel it was born into, the vase cracks and disintegrates.

Certainly one need never stop speaking with the departed just because their body and heart have returned to their respective sources. The heart is the bridge across which we can encourage them to follow their deepest healing, to forgive and allow themselves to be forgiven, to enter the light of their great nature.

There are a series of exercises that are useful for releasing our obsessive identification with the body. They begin with writing our own eulogy, reading it aloud, and still getting a good night's sleep. The next day envisioning our funeral, seeing the open cemetery plot around which the mourners gather, smelling the freshly turned earth, hearing the empty consolations of our loved ones, feeling their grief at losing us. Observe our coffin being lowered into the open earth and notice the feelings and imagery that arise as the first shovels of dirt are tossed onto our casket.

If we want to take this cemetery practice to another level, then visualize our corpse disintegrating in the earth. Picture its skin gradually shrinking then splitting, its muscles and fibers decaying, its bones protruding through the carcass like yesterday's Thanksgiving turkey. Watch our organs slowly petrify then turn to dust as our ribs and thighs rot in a jumble. Watching with clarity and compassion the body compost to its rudimentary elements reminds us that we have a body but certainly are not limited to being just that.

Some years ago, when I was leading a weekly meditation group, many people asked what the single most important quality was to bring into an ill person's room. They were reminded to see that person not as their body, that to reinforce in any way that dying person's misplaced identification was to increase their fear of death and decrease their trust in the process. So, to aid the group to free themselves from their mistaken relationship to the body, we visited the anatomy laboratory at a local university. There we explored a rather pungent six-month-old cadaver that was half-disassembled. Contemplating together the well-displayed muscle layers, the withering organs, and empty brain pan was something of a twentieth-century cemetery meditation.

Those who said afterward that they had an unusual sense of themselves as just an awareness viewing just a body (something of an out-of-that-body experience) were invited to an autopsy. Ondrea and I took many groups to one or another of the hospitals we were associated with to experience a little more of that process. In autopsies they saw that the body was no different from a carcass hanging in a butcher shop window. It was a network of flesh, nerve, ligament, muscle, and bone that stunk when the pathologist opened it to expose its glistening organs. This was a powerful teaching not only in impermanence or the awful truth of the statement that beauty is only skin deep, but in the priorities that make life worth living.

Traditionally, this sort of cemetery meditation was practiced by a yogi camping out next to a rotting corpse, or by monks and nuns who envisioned their body lying on the ground into which it was decomposing. Thus, when we extended the practice to seeing oneself decomposing beneath the ground, I noticed in myself a considerable fear of being buried alive. It was a fierce contemplation, one best not delayed. It allowed me to establish a dialogue with this rudimentary fear that could increasingly be expanded in the primal vastness of soft-belly. It made it no longer necessary to bury alive my fear of being buried alive. It did not diminish the fear so much as it made it accessible to the heart.

The contemplation is the same whether we visualize our body decomposing in or on the earth, or consumed at 2000 degrees in a crematorium oven. (As a Jew I found the latter particularly powerful and helpful for certain difficult levels in my forgiveness practice.) It catches us where we are holding. It reminds us to soften and let go.

Let us go to our grave and look inside. Pick up your worm-eaten skull. Peer into its hollow bowl where the world seemed once to exist, and marvel that, as Tagore said, "So much could stay so long in so little." Watching our body dissolve into the earth is a Rorschach test for our fear of the uncontrollable. It is not easy to relinquish our habitual identifications.

We have closed our body like a fist around the life force attempting to hold it in, to live forever. This limits our courage and generosity and shortens our life. The body has become so cramped from grasping that it may take a while for it to soften into its natural spaciousness. Opening that fist is an act of faith, peeling back our fingers one by one, relinquishing level after level of holding, letting go of the body to free the spirit to live lightly within it.

34

FINDING THE LOTUS BEFORE WINTER

I n a weekend workshop in Los Angeles a few years ago, several of the participants with life-threatening illness who shared their life story as it seemed to be coming to an end had a common theme. They felt that they could not die in peace because they had not fulfilled their ambitions. They had not gotten the brass ring from their repeated spinning on the merry-go-round and it left them dazed and disappointed. It was perhaps all the more poignant because many were out-of-work actors lost in the miasma of Hollywood hell.

One unusually handsome fellow stood particularly erect to say that, in working with his AIDS, the issue he found most upsetting was that after nearly a dozen years of "trying to make it in the film industry" he now saw he was not going to succeed after all. He said that he felt he would not live long enough to be a featured player, that his dream of seeing his name above the title was collapsing with his body. Pale and shaken he spoke of making "the great admission to myself that I was going to die a failure, my dream unrealized." He personified a frightened part of us all. His skeleton seemed unable to support him any longer as he slumped back into his seat. Hardly able to catch his breath, he said he had hoped he would be "one with the process," but instead found himself "beside myself with grief." Feeling that life had not kept its promise, that he had not been up to the task, his deflated ambition bound him like an umbilicus about his throat, strangling the completion of his birth, choking off the fulfillment of his death.

The analogy of his disappointment with "a life of show business" was not missed by most in the audience. His predicament stimulated something in the collective cortex as one person after another stood to say they too feared that if they did not get some accolade from life it might somehow be relegated to the editing room floor. If they did not succeed, get enlightened, become a superstar before death, it would reduce their life story to black-and-white and disallow any possibility of its being viewed in some Cinemax wide-screen format. Having stared at our own story so long, it is difficult to picture the final curtain without at least some audience response.

It is as true in one theater as in the next. I have held many sobbing in meditation retreats whose greatest fear was that they might not get enlightened before they die. Imagining that completion is accomplished through some momentous event rather than as a deep ongoing process of letting go and healing, they literally do not see where they are. Perhaps they do not recognize that their strong desire for some trophy of their worthiness is a trophy of their feelings of unworthiness born of a deeper disappointment. Having not discovered their own great truth, having not received the healing they took birth for,

they have settled for success. Whether their dream was star-
dom or starshine, their book published, their true love found,
or their temper defeated, they believed that their life was incomplete.

I have been with many people on their deathbed who
lamented that they could not die at peace because they felt a
failure. It is an all too common stage we go through to the degree that we were more attached to the objects of life than appreciative of its evolutionary unfolding. Those who push
through that sticky web across the path, that feeling of having
not gotten what they came for before it was time to leave, feel
it was well worth the effort, considering the breadth of the
path opened up ahead. Like any grief, feelings of unworthiness
and failure are not new, but at the point of impending loss they
may become acute. Many decry their misfortune at not "getting theirs," forgetting they've already gotten it and now it is up
to them to make an art of it: to build an altar to the sacred past,
to merge with their heart in the immediate present, to open beyond old knowing to the mysterious future.

To discover what we already possess is to go beyond our
limited idea of who, and even what, we are. Discovering our
true nature is called "finding our lotus" by some. The lotus is
not difficult to find if we know where to look. Lotuses prolifer-
ate in the wild, given their natural environment of compassion-
ate service and nonattachment to the fruits of our labors. They
can often be seen blooming in the hothouse of the meditation
center or the deathbed.

The lotus represents that which rises above fetid waters to
share its unexpected beauty. It is a symbol of liberation from
painful attachment to that through which our life must pass in
order to reach its original light. We nurture our lotus by letting

go of the urgency for imagined accomplishment that stunts its growth. It is said that some walk easily accross the river of death, stepping lightly on their lotuses, while others row their boats guided by its fragrance. Some leap the luminous river on faith. Others just arrive because it was on their way. And some, though they grease their bodies in the manner of the masters and have studied all the books about swimming but have never gone near the river, drown into the next unconscious womb before they are halfway across.

One fellow with cancer spoke of finding his lotus "before winter," of getting healed before the absence of cure turned his body cold. He said he wanted to "complete the course" before he died. So he explored that which had always distracted him from life and was now continuing its momentum into death. He said that right on the other side of his feelings of "not-enoughness" was a remarkable insight. He saw the value of not being able to satisfy his desires. It caused him to discover, like Buddha, the cause of all his suffering. It was not only the impossibility of satisfying every desire, much less keeping it that way, it was not not getting this or that, or losing it the next day. *The cause of suffering was desire itself.*

He saw that it was not in the object of desire that lasting satisfaction resided but in the absence of that desire. He mentioned that when something wanted was received, he noticed a momentary spiking of pleasure and the experience we call satisfaction. But to his surprise the satisfaction did not come from the having but from the momentary flash of getting when the light of his great nature was for a moment no longer obstructed by a mind full of desire. It was the absence of desire which offered that feeling of satisfaction, of temporary completeness. The very nature of desire was one of dissatisfaction with any moment in which the object of desire was not present. Desire lived more in the future than the present. It had a quality of longing rather than being. He saw the mind was doomed to feel something of a failure if it did not comprehend that it is unrequited desire itself, which, like a hungry ghost, always calls out for more. This recognition of the painful nature of desire did not make him desireless but allowed him to treat desire with a new respect. He said that he did not even care if his lotus ever bloomed now that he had found it. This reminded me that one of my teachers used to say once you have turned toward the light it doesn't really matter how far away it seems as long as you keep your eye on it.

As Zen master Kennett-Roshi points out, the source of our greatest satisfaction is to experience completely the source of even our least satisfaction, to meet each with clarity and kindness, to visit deep within consciousness our true self and coax it to the surface. We watch our lotus rise through murky waters, feeling that even if it never breaks the surface this time around, just knowing it exists is immense grace. The root from which it grows is as eternal as our play in time and will sprout once again next spring or whenever we do.

Just as some horticulturists "push" flowers, forcing them to bloom by placing them temporarily in darkness, so the contemplation of death can "push" the blossoming of our lotus.

Find your lotus before winter. Once it has germinated it will continue growing right up through the roof of the world. And perhaps appear in Tim's delightful Eden before becoming the great tree of wisdom that pierces even heaven and disappears into the smile on our original face.

35

ARMANDO AND
THE FLOATING
WORLD

A rmando, though deeply religious, was having difficulty finding his lotus because he was looking for it on solid ground. He attempted to barter with the fears of the mind rather than let go into the unfathomable mysteries of the heart. He could not stop beside such quiet waters unless there was a Holy Man walking on them. He tried always to "be spiritual" instead of leaping faithfully, mindfully, into the flow. He did not trust the process. He never got wet.

He was so disappointed that after years of formal spiritual practice he had not gotten "the big hit" before he died. He felt that he had failed in some way. Forgetful of the kindness he had offered to so many others with AIDS, he was merciless with himself. Trying to force some sense from a senseless world through a brain invaded by CMV (cytomegalovirus), his belly became hard as a gravestone as he whispered in despair on the phone "Oh boy, Stephen, oh boy!" feeling wholly unprepared for what was coming. He had put so much effort into religious ritual and so little into the deep inner work that always needs doing, he reached a momentary hell instead of an eternal heaven.

It was perhaps because of his fear of letting go that he found "the floating world" such a threat. He said that he was afraid of the "floating world" that was encompassing him, that he could not let go into his death because he felt he still needed to "maintain the senses," keep control, die in some officially recognized manner. (It is here perhaps that we can see the shadow that even so great a light as "conscious dying" can produce by creating models in the mind that may obscure an individual's intuition and slow their spiritual momentum with unkind comparisons.)

The floating world is just the ordinary world seen from the increased perspective of the vastness of being. It is a somewhat-out-of-the-world experience, unencumbered by the heaviness produced from the strict limitations of rational thought. In it there are light years between atoms, galaxies in each cell, and a Chagall-like abeyance of gravity that allows each thing to seek its own level. It is the floating world of the senses before they are brought to ground through interpretation and "understanding." But as one patient said, "Our world, no matter how neat and safe we try to make it, is not made up of 'duck pins all-in-a-row'; it's made up of ducks."

Reminded of the many stories he had heard of others having to discard old models in order to reach completion, he was still unable to release the fear that he was unworthy of his idea of God. Like many, he felt he had to be better than he felt he was to enter into the heart of the divine.

I shared with him that his experience of the floating world

was a rich opportunity not unlike that of those in coma, which acts as kind of a mezzanine—you're not on the next floor yet but it offers a whole new perspective of the first floor. When I spoke of the benefits of the "floating world" as an opportunity to rehearse his letting go into something less dense than his suffering, that it was just the same old world a bit lighter and less condensed, thus less difficult to pass through, he sighed wistfully and softened his belly. Speaking of his difficulty with the floating world as not unlike the experiences of people in fever dreams, I relayed to him the story of our daughter many years before frightened by a fever dream in which she felt she was "floating over the house." And how when she was reminded "to look around while you're out there," to count the roof tiles, to let go and float freely through the clouds, her experience changed radically, as she became quite comfortable and intermittently released a giggle. He wept and softened deeper. He died more peacefully than he had often lived, letting go perhaps more through sheer muscle fatigue than from trust. Gradually buoyed up by the floating world into a process so merciful and so long forgotten that I can imagine his relief at its odd beneficence.

36

A GOOD DAY

TO DIE

There is a Native American saying, "Today is a good day to die for all the things of my life are present." This embodies the possibilities of a life reviewed and completed. A life in which even death is not excluded. I am speaking here of a whole death that succeeds a whole life. A life caught up to, and lived in, the present, that rides the breath and knows the power of thought to create the world, experiencing itself in its fullness and emptiness.

The more mindful we are the less there is to crowd us in our deathbed. When we are living our life instead of only thinking it, nothing remains undone, and if we should die that day we are pleased that our death can be so complete. When everything is brought up-to-date, and the heart is turned toward itself, it is a good day to die.

Once opened, our original lotus knows its way home by heart.

Thus, it is suggested that we practice dying (find a perfect day to die) with a very interesting and enjoyable and sometimes frightening exercise called "Taking a Day Off." It is a daylong contemplation of seeing the world without ourselves in it. It speaks to that place within us that asks, How can I not be among you? Some call this practice "Dead for a Day." We walk the streets as though we were not there, as though we had died yesterday. We see the world in our absence. We act as though we were already dead and had this last chance to visit the world we have left behind. We grieve for ourselves and go on.

The power of such an exercise is demonstrated in the popularity of such films as *It's a Wonderful Life*. Something essential is drawn to the surface when we recognize that *This day may be the last day of the rest of our life.*

Experience each breath as though it were the last. Enter each moment, each conversation, each lovemaking, each meal, each prayer, each meditation as though there may never be another.

Just as yesterday we pretended to be dead, today we pretend we are alive. We walk the streets filled with presence. We watch the gratitude at our rapid recovery. We cut out the middleman of death, not needing to die in order to take our next incarnation, we take birth now, in the middle of the street, in the midst of a life redoubled by new birth.

We enter life so fully that even if we died it would not spoil our day.

37

NAME THAT
TUNE

Many indigenous spiritual traditions developed skillful means of preparing for death. For example, at puberty, each young Native American man or woman went into the wilderness on a vision quest and often returned with, among other gifts, a personal healing song that was also used as a death chant. Having practiced their healing/death chant through illness and danger and a lifetime of difficult moments, by the time death actually arrived these people had established a familiar path into the unfamiliar—a sacred path.

There are also many "modern" cultures that practice such artful means of approaching death. In Christianity, our death chants range from the Lord's Prayer to the Jesus Prayer to the Rosary. In Judaism, there is the power of the Shema or perhaps from the bar mitzvah quest a line in Hebrew that always touched the heart. In Buddhism, we chant "*Gate* [pronounced 'gatay'], *gate, paragate, parasamgate, bodhi svaha!*"—which is loosely translated as "Gone, gone, gone beyond, altogether gone beyond, altogether free at last!" It is chanted in monasteries and graveyards. And the wisest among us perhaps chant it beneath our breath at births as well, knowing that neither birth nor death will free us but only a letting go into our original light. In Hinduism, we wish to die with "Ram," one of the names of God, on our lips.

A death chant can act as a refuge from the storm, or an open window to the sun. Mantras or prayers cultivated in sincere spiritual practice work very well for many. Some recite scripture when danger approaches. Some whisper lullabies on their deathbed. Many, as did the vision questers, trust their heart to reveal the song. They listen closely and discover they knew it all along. Our participation in the song depends on a willingness, an openness, to the fluency of the heart. Actually, the fanciful imaginings and hero rehearsals of our famous last words are the first faltering steps toward uncovering a healing death chant. Some people begin there, repeating their imagined last words almost like a mantra, watching it change and evolve into something less theatrical, less the panache of a flourished exit, more the slow gentility of our humble opening to the unknown. I have seen many begin their life review and end their life with the same sweet song, repeating, "I love you, I love you, I love you," on their deathbed. A few with their last breaths have sung "Row, row, row your boat." One old Bostonian kept saying, "Here today and gone tomorrow." One woman, having completed her work, repeated gently, "Sun sun; done done."

The benefits of developing a heart song/death chant are unmistakable. Thus, as part of the "dying experiment," it is suggested we find and cultivate our own personal healing/death chant over the next year. Develop a refuge that gets stronger with use.

Sit quietly in the heart and listen. If no song comes to mind settle into the state of patience. In fact, if we never found a song but developed instead the timeless spaciousness of patience, it might support us just as well on our deathbed. Audition lines as they arise. See which remain when the others are forgotten. Experiment.

Part of finding our lotus is to uncover our song. Begin singing daily (a powerful way of letting go) whatever song presents itself, whether gospel or rock and roll, and let the heart do the rest. For some the song changes every few months throughout the year. But everyone, no matter what the song, discovers over time that the secret of chanting is in the listening, not the voicing, and a circuit is completed between the mind and heart that opens intuition and gently increases the volume of "the still small voice within." Whatever the chant is it will bring us closer to grace, our original nature, the Kingdom of Heaven that is within.

If we think we'll just skip this particular exercise because it's kind of embarrassing to sing, think how disconcerting a death unaccompanied by the heart might be.

After listening to some of my life review tales, Ondrea bought me a new conga drum so that I might reexplore the delights of my early years as a musician. And I did, and played and sang without inhibition, making a joyful sound unto the sacred vastness, which I had not been able to do so many years before, feeling that my song was unworthy to offer God.

If you would like to tune more profoundly to the place from which this song arises, study the works of the devotional poets, Rumi, Kabir, and Mirabai.

38

AGING

At fifty-eight I hear people turning thirty complain about their aging. Less stamina, they say, and more flatulence. Tennis elbow and new glasses. At forty they struggle against the body. Nutritional supplements and sit-ups. At fifty they feel defeated. Aging, for that part of each of us that identifies with an agile body and an unforgetful mind, is loss. In our resistance to change we are overlooking one of the greatest preparations of all for death, and one of the great teachings in impermanence.

Aging teaches us to follow our life force inward. It is an object lesson in how awareness is gradually drawn toward the center, as in death, leaving the extremities (including the outer senses) to fend for themselves. Perhaps that's why so many people of advanced years speak of feeling like youngsters in their heart.

The gradual decline of the body is fascinating. It is a slow cemetery meditation. It's our reflection in the funeral parlor window. It reminds us how short life may be and how sweet it might become.

The body takes about seven years to replace all its cells. As we age original factory parts get harder to come by. We accept seconds and rebuilds. Some are even transplanted with recycled parts. We get less miles to the gallon, and eventually, after several towings, we must abandon the body by the side of the road. From there we must go the rest of the way alone with just our heart for guidance.

To further examine the potential for conscious aging, see the forthcoming book by Ram Dass.

39

DECEMBER

As we turned over the last page on the calendar, Ondrea and I looked into each other's eyes and said good-bye, our hearts resonating with gratitude for the teachings—pleasant and unpleasant—that our lives had offered. Although the yearlong experiment is just a skillful illusion, a dream capable of awakening us from our dream, we noticed a certain grieving at the thought that our lives were nearing their hypothetical end.

Before my eyes even opened on the second of the month, I could feel the trembling. Fear had begun to tally up its losses. It was compiling a death inventory, a loss sheet. I looked about the room and recognized that everything I surveyed that had once given me pleasure could now become an object of pain. The prospect of leaving my well-constructed life behind thickened the air. Being nuzzled by our morning-eager dogs and with a brand-new sun above the snowcapped mountains, it was impossible to ignore how delightful it could be to be alive and how completely that life had to be relinquished. Bounties pleasant to receive but painful to return. Anticipatory grief.

Clearly it was time for final preparations. So I began experimenting a little more with the *phowa* practice we had been developing throughout the year. *Phowa* is the Tibetan Buddhist art and science of consciousness transference that is capable of liberating the life force from the body. It is a concentrated raising of the spirit (experienced as a vibratory cloud of energetic sensation that becomes more distinct as the process, and our concentration, continues) from the abdomen up through the heart and the long tunnel of the throat, then up through the brow and out the top of the head, where it is projected into an image of light visualized above. Some Tibetan monks employing this powerful practice were said to "drop their bodies" before the Chinese invaders' firing squads could pull their triggers.

Phowa is a practice capable of clearing the conduit through which the life force travels on its most skillful exit from the body. Apparently, when perfected, it is capable of initiating a conscious death. It is a "gathering of the light" within the heavy body that rises to join something yet lighter just beyond. Traditionally, the life force is transferred to some deeply respected visualized image of the sacred, whether it be Buddha, Jesus, Mary, or simply our original luminosity seen as a great sphere of light just above our heads. I find working directly with the light itself, as itself, cuts through a lot of conceptual distortion.

In seeking a simple application of this rather complex traditional Tibetan practice, we found it quite natural to join certain elements of *phowa* with the enormous potential for completion and release offered by progressive "energy-center" meditations. These energy centers are called chakras in one tradition and levels of consciousness in another. Some simply view them as states of mind that lead to states of being. This combination of practices results in an "ascension meditation," which opens a channel to the higher levels of consciousness that intensify life and can be utilized at the time of death. We refer to it humorously as an "early riser's meditation." Fear that this kind of meditation accelerates death is unfounded; opening practices like these enrich our birth.

As our version of energy-center meditation/*phowa* developed, we noticed to our delight how all the previous practices came into alignment. Beginning from the energy center in the belly the light of consciousness is on one level visualized and on another experienced as sensation. It is sensed collecting in the belly. The resulting openness is then encouraged to practice loving kindness, breathing in and out of the heart that draws the light upward as it grows in intensity. Sending waves of mercy and compassion into each aspect of the mind and body, we observe a quieting as some deeper presence gathers to depart. A sense of expanding space continues upward, illuminating all that has remained unsaid in the dark passage of the throat. (This is perhaps the tunnel so many speak of traversing on their way into death.) The song learned long ago from our rising lotus is sung to clear the way and propel us upward through the brow in which resides what is called by some the "third eye" and only half-jokingly by others "our sacred Cyclops." This is considered by many a seer as actually our "good" eye, the only one that can see beyond our conditioned ways of seeing. It is, of course, a knowing eye not a seeing eye. It is the eye through which we look within to experience the universe unfolding. It is the single eye that concentrates duality into the One: the eye of insight, the locus of the point of remembrance on the ascent into death, as well as the point of forgetfulness on the descent into birth.

That cloud of energy, sensed at first in the belly, becomes

intensified as it gradually rises through the energy centers of the mind/body, until it is articulated as a shimmering light that emanates through the top of the head like a sparkling fountain. Our brightening light expands as it rises into the vast sphere of white light floating just above the open caldera where the crown of our skull used to be. This is the path of *phowa* as it travels through the body and out again.

Even after a long cultivation of the separate meditations that link together to create the process, this is no simple task. Each time one practices this *phowa* a bit more is understood about the next step. It can take hours for even a fleeting glimpse of its potential. Some spend at least a half hour at each energy center. There are five to be opened and traversed. As one practitioner said of her growing *phowa* practice, "Don't wait until you hear the train in the distance to get on track."

In the course of *phowa* practice I noticed after a month or so a blockage in my throat perhaps from the unexpressed grief of working so many years with the dying. I therefore stopped the "upward practice" and started to chant and sing each day for about two months until my throat felt clear: one of my teacher's favorite mantras in the morning, and perhaps "You are the sunshine of my heart" in the afternoon. It was another example of how having a year to prepare was very skillful.

As *phowa* practice evolves it begins to gather a light in the belly, which may also be experienced as a particular sensation, and moves upward through a conduit made wider by practice and surrender. It rises from the heart to the brow through the corridors of speech humming its life song. Passing through the enormous vistas just between the eyes, it melts the crown of the skull and breaks free like an uncaged bird soaring into a boundless sky.

Though my *phowa* practice is still in its infancy, there is a sense of the grace that awaits. If I should die this moment that which might previously have resisted such a gathering and release of the light might now swing wide the door for its safe passage. As the practice continues to develop it may take less effort to rise from a soft-belly into the heart of Jesus, to hear the song of Mary, and to enter the clear mind of the Buddha, on our way into a buoyancy of the spirit.

In fact, every once in a while, in a moment of stillness, I would hear what one dying patient referred to as "the orchestra tuning up," an opening into the symphony that wafts in from the floating world. An oddly familiar melody that resonates between form and formlessness, whose notes are perfectly juxtaposed like the stone gardens in space we call "galaxies." Perhaps it is the song the lotus rises above the surface to hear.

And on the day before the last, in the midst of the enormous lullaby, I thought to myself, "We should only be so lucky as to die in this incredible spaciousness and peace." Then, turning toward the mystery, I let go into the floating world, and followed my heart into the luminous unknown, the body light as a feather, a sense of ease pervading as I felt myself borne into the vastness of original being, knowing that love was the only rational act of a lifetime.

EPILOGUE

A year after the completion of my one-year experiment, benefits continue to accrue. In the course of resolving unfinished business and tidying up loose ends, my life has opened in subtle and unexpected ways. My sense of time has changed—there seems to be more of the present. A newfound energy has been liberated in the course of the life review as that part of the life force once dedicated to suppressing the mind and numbing the heart has been emancipated. My relationships with friends has deepened and, in some cases, blossomed again. Afflictive emotions, particularly to do with the past, have become considerably less cumbersome. And love is more available and sustainable. It feels as though I have made peace with my life. With these changes has come a renewed dedication to priorities, which makes the path ahead particularly clear.

Ironically, after I have spent a year practicing dying, the quality most noticeably enhanced is a new joy in life. This refreshing lightness of spirit is reinforced by increasingly clear insight, a deeper appreciation, and a broader acceptance of things as they are, which arises within an expanded sense of presence.

Perhaps because this book was written as though it were the last I would ever write, and because its benefits are so immediately and intuitively recognizable, this has been the easiest and most enjoyable book process I have yet experienced and the shortest book that wanted to be written.

Appendix

GROUP

PRACTICE

Although it has not been my intention to schedule anyone's last year, since I have been sharing this process in workshops, many "Year to Live" groups have begun to spring up and have requested some sort of syllabus for a yearlong group process.

Some attempt at such a month-to-month progression follows with the proviso that, of course, all of the processes, from the life review, to a deepening introspection on our death, to the investigation of practices such as noting and meditation for the development of depth consciousness, begin to drop seeds and take root from the moment the heart ponders this experiment.

FIRST MONTH

All members of the group read the book and share important passages with each other. Explore the value of a one-year commitment to consciousness and healing. Make a note of the day you begin the process. This will be your experimental "due date" one year hence. Reflect on what your reactions/responses might be to receiving a one-year prognosis. Explore this in terms of life changes, new projects, and the mechanics and grace of dealing with unfinished business. This is when to begin the journal. As the months go by, watch how the practices gradually change and deepen both in the journal and in the heart.

SECOND MONTH

Explore what it means to begin preparing for death. Establish the practices of opening to the unknown and facing fear. Begin to explore the group's experience and concepts of dying and death as two discrete subjects. Start work on the fear of dying, the fear of death, and the fear of fear itself. Soft-belly practice for fifteen minutes twice a day. At the end of each month, if it feels appropriate, read aloud some of the previous month's journal entries.

THIRD MONTH

Each day become more fully alive. Practice noting gently and nonjudgmentally throughout the day. Add mindfulness practice to soft-belly opening work: fifteen minutes soft-belly and twenty minutes watching the breath, noting the activities of the mind. Approach illness as an experiment in staying present, in opening your heart in hell. Discuss how we fear our hidden pain even more than death, and how noting and mindfulness brings that pain to the surface where it can be healed.

FOURTH MONTH

Practice the dying meditation both in the group and individually. Watch the fear of pain, the fear of nonbeing, the fear of Judgment Day. Deepen the discussion about dying, death, and what might come afterward. Share how the process is going for each member of the group. Wake each morning as if it were your last day on earth.

FIFTH MONTH

Intensify life review practice. Increase casual as well as formal reflection on the events and people of the past. Practice daily forgiveness and gratitude meditations in relationship to both pleasant and unpleasant memories. Listen for your life song among the insights that hum through the mind. Increase the time you spend in meditation to an hour a day, if possible. Make peace with your life.

SIXTH MONTH

If individual members of the group have not already built an altar, they should do so now. Dedicate a corner of a room or even a whole room to the processes of your life. This is a place to refine and deepen the life review, a place worthy of dying in. By the end of the month begin some sort of volunteer work to offer service to others. Build a group altar. Six months have been completed: more time passed than remaining.

SEVENTH MONTH

Who dies? Investigate that which remains when the body has fallen away, as well as that which was present before we took birth. Occasionally add original-face meditation to those meditations already being practiced. Keep company with the wise, reading together the writings and listening to the recordings of those whose spiritual practice is so well developed that they have received and can share insights into the nature of the after-death experience: Ramana Maharshi, Nisargadatta, Buddha, Jesus, Sarada Devi, the Hassidim, Aldous Huxley, Ram Dass, Dogen, Ananda Mayi Ma, and Neem Karoli Baba (known as Maharaji).

EIGHTH MONTH

Explore attitudes to and the possibilities of reincarnation. Practice letting-go meditation, holding nowhere so that our deepest truth can arise spontaneously. Discuss the common dreams that connect the departed with the grieving. Experiment with rebirth using the first breath/last breath exercise.

NINTH MONTH

Add sweeping meditation in order to fully inhabit the body. Consider how the body will be disposed of. Examine how to sweep up after yourself. Discuss the nature of the impermanent, often uncomfortable, body into which we have incarnated. Add cemetery meditation to your basic practice for a month. In your journal inquire into the nature of being and becoming.

TENTH MONTH

Write a will, a memorial service, and an epitaph, and read them to the group. Experiment with making videotapes, and writing letters and poems for those who will remain behind. Watch whatever anticipatory grief arises as the year nears its end. Try "Dead for a Day" practice. Envision the distribution of your precious possessions. Note that some receive a place of honor while others disappear into the back of a closet. In your heart release your belongings (the one with the most toys has the most to let go of), and even more painfully, release your belonging (your family, your friends, your socially approved identity). Living consciously allows an appreciation of each thing in its time. Extend letting-go practice to half an hour a day.

ELEVENTH MONTH

Dedicate more time to family and friends. Recognize that they, like you, are constantly being swept away by the stream of impermanence. Start a group project for the needy. If possible visit an AIDS ward, a ward for burned children, a home for the aging. Recognize that mishap is not a punishment from God but simply an event that can be used as a teaching in mercy and self-awareness. Explore the difference beween pity and compassion. Recognize that even good works done well will not keep illness, old age, and death away, that God and the nature of things will not and need not protect us. We have already inherited all we need to survive our death with our heart open and our mind focused on the brilliance of our original nature.

TWELFTH MONTH

Begin to concentrate on the outgoing aspect of the body-sensation sweeping practice. Bring your attention to the top of the head as often as possible. Become familiar with the subtle sensations of the scalp. Follow the sensations into the space above the head. Practice with joy and a sense of renewed investigation into what it is that dies and what it is that doesn't. Practice lightly and with a growing openness to the unknown. Make room for the truth to present itself, as it will, and don't hold on to that either.

This is the last month of the rest of your life. Combine practices. Say good-bye to loved ones in the center of your heart. Thank your body for its perseverance under difficult circumstances, and have mercy on it when it pleads to be released from pain. With kindness and clarity say farewell to this life and prepare for the renewal of death.

At the end of the year disband the group. Those who wish to continue the process of consciousness exploration may form a new "after-death" group.

ABOUT THE AUTHOR

Stephen Levine is a poet and teacher of guided meditation and healing techniques that have found widespread application over the last twenty years. His best-selling books in the United States and Europe (including *Who Dies?*, *Healing into Life and Death*, *A Gradual Awakening*, and with his wife and spiritual partner, Ondrea, *Embracing the Beloved*) are considered groundbreaking in their field.

Many of the meditations and techniques suggested in this book are available on audiotape from:

Warm Rock Tapes
P.O. Box 108
Chamisal, NM 87521
1-800-731-HEAL